DIPLOMACY AT SEA

DIPLOMACY AT SEA

James Cable

Naval Institute Press

Published and distributed in the
United States of America and Canada in 1985 by
THE NAVAL INSTITUTE PRESS
Annapolis, Maryland 21402

Library of Congress Catalog Card No. 84–42617

ISBN 0–87021–836–0

Printed in Hong Kong

For Viveca as always

Contents

Preface

The dozen essays in this book are a selection from a range of similar productions over the last dozen years. Their common concern is with a particular aspect of international relations and naval affairs: disputes as a cause of conflict and the resolution of conflict by methods short of war.

The first and longest of these essays – 'Coercion, Compromise and Compliance' – states the theme and discusses the nature and prevalence of coercive diplomacy. Other essays offer illustrative variations, particularly in relation to the threat or use of naval force in support of diplomacy. The relationship between theory and practice is also explored, as is the regrettably declining role of traditional diplomacy. Cant and the thriller have been chosen as examples of the curious cultural basis of many political assumptions and of the surprising and only partly conscious roots of much political strife.

All but the first of these essays have appeared previously. The author is grateful to the following editors and publishers for permission to reprint them here: the Editor of *International Relations* for 'The Diffusion of Maritime Power' (1982) and 'Diplomacy: a Case for Resuscitation' (1983); the Editor of *International Affairs* for 'The Useful Art of International Relations' (1981) and 'Interdependence: a Drug of Addiction?' (1983); the Editor of *Navy International* for 'Will Gibraltar be Next?' (1982) and 'Hong Kong: a Base without a Fleet' (1983); the Editor of *United States Naval Institute Proceedings* for 'The Falklands Conflict' (1982); the Editor of *Encounter* for 'Surprise in the Falklands' (1982); the Editor of the *Journal of the Royal United Services Institute for Defence Studies* for 'Surprise and the Single Scenario' (1983); Chatto and Windus Ltd for 'Cant in Foreign Policy' (originally published as Chapter 1 of *Appearance and Reality in International Relations*, by Grant Hugo, 1970); the Editor of *The Contemporary Review* for 'The Political Influence of the Thriller' (by Grant Hugo, 1972).

Some minor alterations have been made to earlier versions to remove misprints, to restore the original text, or for stylistic reasons, but never to allow hindsight to correct any flaws in the author's prescience.

No systematic attempt has been made to reconcile, or to contrast, the views expressed in these pages with the received opinions of the academic community. Although reading has contributed as much as personal experience, the author has been more concerned to present his own ideas than to distil the wisdom of others. References have accordingly been kept to the necessary minimum.

1 Coercion, Compromise and Compliance

COERCION IN INTERNATIONAL RELATIONS

Coercion is implicit in most aspects of international relations as it is in most human relationships. Between parents and children; employers and workers; trade unions and their members; officials (even the humblest) and citizens: wishes are normally expressed as orders or demands. The phrasing may be polite and the penalties of disobedience not even hinted at, but the assumption is clear: some people are entitled to expect compliance. An equal relationship, in which proposals are advanced for discussion on their merits, is the exception rather than the rule. Even in commercial transactions on the allegedly free market, it is a matter of everyday experience that anyone in a position to do so, from the tycoon to the shop assistant, will seek to impose his own conditions for buying and selling goods and services, whether or not these conditions are actually to his commercial advantage. 'Any colour you like, as long as it's black', is an attitude that the ordinary citizen encounters at every step he takes and irrespective of the level of the transaction. To anyone able to exercise it the power of coercion is intrinsically desirable.

Naturally such assumptions of divine right, even by insurance companies, do not always pass unchallenged. Obstinate individuals will occasionally put the implied power of coercion to the test. Sometimes they will expose it as a bluff; more often reach a compromise. But, if the relationship is genuinely unequal, they must usually fall back on a reluctant compliance. Individual victories over government departments, major commercial concerns or important trade unions are rare and often expensive.

In international relations the same principles apply, but with one important difference. The real possibilities of coercion are less symmetrically distributed among different states than they are within any particular state. In most states society is so organised as actually

1

to facilitate the exercise of coercion by those who are recognised as possessing power, whether this power is political, administrative, economic or the result of organised cooperation. 'In England', as it was once said on high legal authority, 'justice is open to all, like the Ritz hotel.' In Russia, or in many other countries, there may be no Ritz, but the principle is the same: those who enjoy power, however much they may compete among themselves, have a common interest in maintaining the effectiveness of power against those who lack it.

In the anarchy of international society this is not the case. Even the strongest are ready to risk exalting the humble and meek, if the process seems likely to damage their rivals. As for those governments who enjoy only a little power, a local power, they seldom regard their privileges as depending on the maintenance of respect for the wider claims of more potent governments. On the contrary, they often have cause to believe that even their limited power is significantly related to the degree of independence manifested in its exertion. They are less often content than their equivalents in domestic society to accept their proper station in any obvious hierarchy of power, not even ready to apply themselves seriously to the task of improving, step by small and patient step, their relative position in that hierarchy. Some of them prefer a distinctly protestant approach, assert the equality of sovereign states and claim no less validity for aspirations than for capacities.

They are fortified in these otherwise rather unrealistic notions by two awkward factors which distinguish international society from that of most (but by no means all) nation-states. The first is that, in contemporary international society, power lacks the legitimacy it usually enjoys nationally. At the beginning of the present century, for instance, the concept of European prestige produced a basic minimum of solidarity among the Great Powers and commanded a degree of respect from the weaker nations of other continents that has no equivalent today. Even against a Super Power a countervailing power is now available if not always effective. The second is the superior efficacy of violence as an equaliser. Violence is not, of course, unknown in the domestic society of most states, where its threat or use often proves to be the decisive instrument of social change. There, however, violence is usually marginal. It may tip an uncertain balance of power, but it seldom enables the weak to prevail against the strong, unless the latter are not merely disunited but actually demoralised. In the world at large this factor has a higher value in the general equation. In the absence of any organised system to maintain the illusion that power commands intrinsic authority, the influence of power is critically dependent on its ability to exert appropriate force about a given point. As Chapter 2, admittedly concerned only with the use of power at or from the sea, demonstrates, capacity for the exercise of appropriate force is unevenly distributed and more closely related to the circumstances of particular disputes than to any comparison of aggregate resources.

Actual violence is naturally not a necessary feature of coercion. Force can be less crudely employed and there are many ways in which it can be threatened. Warships, for instance, can easily be deployed in international waters, can pose and maintain a threat without commitment and, if need be, can withdraw as quietly as they came. Economic, financial or administrative pressures are sometimes effective. Even threats are not essential. Much coercion is implicit. If a particular government is generally regarded as able and willing both to reward friends and to punish enemies, its wishes will at least receive more careful consideration. In a dependent relationship between two states, such as that discussed in Chapter 3, the client will be still more attentive to the views of the patron. Even weaker states often enjoy a limited and local leverage over the strong. And the most paradoxical form of coercion is that exercised by some governments with a reputation for irresponsibility or instability. They must be pandered to lest they change sides or collapse. When one government makes a proposal to another, the outcome is less often determined by the intrinsic merits of the proposal than by the answer to that essential question: Who? Whom?

Implicit coercion is the bread and butter of diplomacy. It is the business of diplomats, at home or abroad, to recognise the existence of this factor in international relations and to analyse its strength and direction. Where a coercive relationship favours their own government they may, with the necessary assistance of other agents of the state, be actively concerned in maintaining and fortifying it. They must often rely on it for the success of their representations. In a sophisticated relationship, of course, they try to do so indirectly. Between the United States and Britain, for instance, or the Soviet Union and Finland, it is usually British and Finnish officials who explain to their own governments the disadvantages of refusing some American or Russian request. Direct threats are as rare in implicit coercion as overt acts. Even a reference to feeling in Congress or a pseudonymous article in *Pravda* are the exception rather than the rule. Between any pair of states there is a potential relationship of implied coercion, of which the value, and even the direction, may vary considerably from one time and one cause of dispute to another. Actual disputes are often avoided if this factor is similarly perceived by both sides, but the avoidance of disputes is not the only task of diplomacy. Disputes must sometimes be prosecuted and, if so, ought also to be resolved. There too the coercion factor is important.

Reliance on a relationship of implicit coercion for the routine transactions of normal diplomacy is not, of course, at all the same as coercive diplomacy. The identical element may be present in both, but the distinguishing characteristic of coercive diplomacy is its resort to direct threats and even to overt acts. This often, though not invariably, has the further consequence of removing the dispute from the closed circuit of confidential exchanges to an open arena exposed to the cross winds of public opinion, of heightened emotion and of considerations of national prestige. Publicity alone, however, is not the distinguishing factor. Spanish claims to Gibraltar (further considered in Chapter 4) have been publicly declared for centuries, but Spanish diplomacy, in modern times at least, did not assume a coercive character until actual pressure on the Colony (first applied in 1954) was threatened. What had hitherto been a routine diplomatic dispute within an established pattern of implicit coercion was now transformed by the express challenge of overt acts. One cause, of course, was the diminished credibility of Britain's implicit coercion. Such changes, often described in Moscow as alterations in the correlation of forces in the world, frequently prompt a resort to coercive diplomacy by governments who regard a shift in the general balance of power as either favouring or even demanding a more specific threat of force. Coercive diplomacy, however, has flourished even in eras or situations where relationships of implicit coercion were clearly established: in China during the twenties and thirties, for instance, or in Central America to this day. It is employed not only when the conditions for implicit coercion have changed, but also when this expedient fails to produce the desired result.

It is coercive diplomacy – its characteristics, the occasions for its employment and the conditions for its success – that is the primary subject of this book. Nevertheless it has been necessary to begin by setting it in context, to demonstrate the importance of coercion in all aspects of international relations, to make it clear that coercive diplomacy is only a special case of a more general trend. Coercive diplomacy is the expedient of governments who have attempted other measures without success and also of those governments to whom other measures were not available. A potential capacity for its application is also one of the qualifications for the exercise of implicit coercion. Coercive diplomacy is not the last resort – that is war – but it comes fairly low on the preferential list. It is seldom considered if other expedients appear at all promising.

COMPROMISE IN INTERNATIONAL RELATIONS

It seems natural to regard compromise as the method of first choice for the avoidance of disputes. This is not in fact the case. It is usually difficult to envisage the nature of compromise before the opposing positions have been stated and the dispute has begun. Most politicians, particularly but by no means exclusively in insular Britain, experience genuine difficulty in imagining the existence of foreign views radically different from their own. This deficiency ought to be remedied by their own diplomats, but, for the reasons explained in Chapter 5, the fundamentally different nature of foreigners must usually be experienced to be appreciated. Moreover, even the best-informed efforts to shortcircuit this process tend to be counter-productive. If one government begins by advancing what it genuinely considers a compromise proposal, this is normally taken by the other side as a maximum objective requiring erosion if national self-respect is to be maintained. At best an initial compromise is likely to impair the negotiating position of the government that advances it. At worst, particularly insofar as it is perceived by the adversary as a compromise, it suggests a lack of confidence and resolution that makes any compromise seem unnecessary.

Compromise, moreover, is seldom simply a matter of finding a middle way between conflicting aspirations. It must also reflect some measure of agreement on the relative opportunities for coercion enjoyed by the two sides. This is all the more important because many disputes are not concerned with different applications or interpretations of the same principle, but with the clash of two incompatible principles. In the Falklands dispute, for instance, which is considered in Chapters 6 and 7, Argentina advanced claims to territorial sovereignty which Britain answered by arguments about the rights and wishes of the inhabitants. The chances of the compromising equation were much diminished because the two sides were using different and incompatible integers. This was nevertheless not the factor which determined the Argentine resort to coercive diplomacy, nor the British choice of war as their response. The discrepant priorities assigned to land or to people were difficult to resolve, but not impossible. What turned dispute into conflict was a radically different assessment of the chances of coercion.

In Buenos Aires misleading notions were actually promoted by the long British quest for compromise. This was obviously not prompted by acceptance of the Argentine case and none of the proposals advanced could be objectively regarded as offering substantial satisfaction to Argentine claims to sovereignty (which means unfettered control). Yet concessions unwelcome to the islanders and to British public opinion were increasingly dangled before the Argentine negotiators. Why? The answer could surely only be that the British thought the coercive balance, which they were making no visible efforts to maintain, was tilting against them. It must, in Buenos Aires, have been a seductive argument that the hesitant British, so resistant to rational argument, would nevertheless acquiesce in a *fait accompli*: that one bold push would do the trick.

That, of course, is one of the snags about coercive diplomacy: if it does not succeed, it often aggravates the dispute. This is a consideration requiring further discussion, but the immediate issue is the crucial importance of timing to the success of compromise as a diplomatic expedient. The terms discussed before the Argentine invasion of 2 April 1982, even, more dubiously, during the rest of that month, lost their relevance once hostilities were seriously engaged. The coercive balance had not changed. Further weeks of combat would be needed before contrasting perceptions of that balance finally coincided. The nature of the dispute was nevertheless fundamentally altered by the Argentine exercise of coercive diplomacy on 2 April 1982. That ruled out compromise in any customary use of the term. Thereafter the most that could seriously be expected was some diplomatic softening of the harsh reality of compliance – by one side or the other.

Compromise is essentially an intermediary expedient. It can scarcely be attempted before the dispute has begun, but its prospects decline as the temperature rises; the very factor which makes it more desirable and less attainable. It resolves more disputes than it ever avoids.

COMPLIANCE IN INTERNATIONAL RELATIONS

Compliance is often regarded as an entirely pacifist, even Christian, expedient in international relations: turning the other cheek. This is an exaggerated view. Admittedly compliance with unwelcome demands can seem distinctly Christian when the alternative is war, but arguments of rational self-interest are often available to support ethical considerations. Compliance, which means yielding to coercion, often seems, sometimes proves to be, the sensible course. If the only true alternative is the kind of total war that nobody, least of all Britain, could hope to win, compliance may well appear as the one sane option in a mad world.

Unfortunately, even in those extreme cases when a government is confronted with an option of disasters, the choice is seldom either obvious or clear-cut. On 14 October 1939, for instance, Stalin and Molotov handed to the Finnish Ambassador a memorandum proposing various cessions of Finnish territory to the Soviet Union (and rather larger cessions of Soviet territory to Finland), the establishment of a Soviet base and Soviet forces in Finnish territory and the mutual suppression of frontier fortifications. These proposals had been brewing for many months and Field Marshal Mannerheim, whose patriotism was as unquestionable as his ideological commitment, had earlier recommended compliance with a milder variant as militarily preferable to the alternative of a hopeless war with the Soviet Union. Even the compromise he later favoured was nevertheless rejected by the Finnish Government, whose successors were compelled, after two defeats in war, to accept much worse terms.

A revisionist school of historians and other writers has subsequently emerged in Finland to argue that, in 1939, compliance would have been less disadvantageous to Finland. The controversy thus excited does not lend itself to objective resolution, but it illustrates the discrepant influence on choice of the assessment of intentions as opposed to capacities, of political and of military considerations. Mannerheim was obviously right to believe that compliance would not significantly have reduced Finland's chances of withstanding the Soviet Union in war. These were, whatever Finland decided, negligible. He was equally correct, at that time, in discounting Finland's prospects of receiving effective military assistance from other powers. The crucial question, however, concerned the political impact of Finnish compliance, both domestically and on the Soviet Union.

Would compliance have invited further demands and initiated a process culminating, as it did in the Baltic States, in reabsorption into the Russian Empire? Did the defiance of 1939 give Finland a reputation, as one of those wicked animals which defends itself when attacked, that now accounts for its surprising independence? Or would the Soviet Union have been content with Finnish acceptance, in

1939, of what subsequently turned out to be proposals of little practical advantage to the Soviet Union, and would they have extended to a submissive Finland the same tolerance as that shown, after 1945, to an animal now docile, but of established intransigence, even ferocity? There are many arguments, mostly by analogy, on either side and no certain answer is possible. But the notion that compliance is habit-forming at home and abroad encourages the expectation of similar responses to further demands, is at least tenable. There have been many examples since the first payment of Danegeld in those distant years when the Long Ships exerted their coercive diplomacy on England's undefended coasts. A reputation for resistance in extremity may, on the other hand, prove the best basis for a policy of compliance in the less demanding exigencies of routine diplomacy.

Such extreme cases are, however, too various in their circumstances and in their results to support any general conclusions about the utility of compliance. Very many nations, in the last fifty years, have been threatened with war by superior enemies or have even suffered surprise attack (on which see Chapter 8). The record of these events offers examples of most conceivable responses to mortal challenge, but it is hard to discern any convincing relationship between the nature of the reaction and the eventual result. Defiance arguably proved advantageous to Finland, but so did compliance to Denmark. Different lessons might, however, be drawn from the defiance shown by South Vietnam or from the repeated compliance of Czechoslovakia. And, in many cases, both expedients were attempted at different dates and with results that elude objective definition. Some countries never had a real choice. Who in the Lebanon, for instance, could have avoided quarter of a century of bitter conflict by complying with whose wishes? It is not difficult, in the context of international relations, to compare the fate of some nations with that of pensioners, the sick, orphans, the aged, the unemployed and the indigent, who suffer from domestic disputes in which they can exert no coercion, can attempt no compromise and are denied all opportunity for compliance, because they are merely victims and not parties to the dispute.

Compliance, no less than coercion or compromise, is not a magic formula. Its utility depends on the circumstances in which it is to be employed. Where the relationship is one of implicit coercion it can, however, be argued that compliance is the most reliable expedient for the avoidance of disputes. This has been a principle of Finland's very successful foreign policy for nearly forty years. It is, of course, an exacting expedient. Its implications were well defined by President Kekkonen, when contrasting his own 'active' policy with the more 'passive' stance of his predecessor, President Paasikivi.

> As far as I understand he had adopted the habit of first resisting strongly, and then, when there was no other way out, he made the necessary compromises. In my opinion confidence must be won by seeking suitable forms of cooperation on one's own and not merely by waiting for suggestions from the other side.[1]

The cost to Finland of this policy of active compliance has been much exaggerated in Western countries. Most European members of NATO, for instance, have had to make greater material concessions to the United States. There are no Soviet military bases or forces on Finnish soil, nor is Finland expected to sacrifice contracts, join in embargoes or boycotts, send forces outside her own country, increase her defence expenditure or run risks to support Soviet foreign policy. Finnish domestic policies have been unaffected as has her flourishing market economy. The price paid by Finland is an extreme and nation-wide deference to Soviet susceptibilities. As Russians are thin-skinned and have an oriental appetite for flattery, anyone in Finnish public life is constrained to a degree of tact sometimes regarded by impatient foreigners as a fawning hypocrisy. It is a policy only possible to a people exceptionally tough, self-disciplined, realistic and united in their determination to preserve their national independence. Active compliance (which naturally includes discreet resistance to any encroachment on core values) has worked well for Finland, but is perhaps better not attempted by nations more favourably situated or which have never proved themselves in the isolated defiance of a Winter War.

Nevertheless, if Finland is an extreme and exceptional case, there are many countries exposed to implicit coercion who occasionally rely on active compliance to anticipate unwelcome requests. Because their policies are less consistent in this respect, they are more often the victims of coercive diplomacy. This they sometimes successfully resist. You pay your money and you take your choice. Coercion, compromise and compliance are all options appropriate to different disputes. Even to a Super Power the first is not always available and the weakest state may sometimes find a viable alternative to compliance. In international relations circumstances alter cases.

ALTERNATIVE EXPEDIENTS

To many readers analysis of international relations in terms of coercion, compromise and compliance will seem inadequate, narrow, even sourly pessimistic. What about cooperation, joint endeavour, collective security, shared values, friendship among ordinary people, the common interests of the human race? Where are arms control, the peace movement, even the United Nations and international law?

Some of these considerations certainly deserve a glance, but a harder look must first be taken at a factor of more universal and enduring importance: cant. The illustrations in Chapter 9 can be supplemented by more recent examples. The Finnish policy of active compliance, for instance, is never officially so described. On the contrary it reflects the deep mutual understanding and friendship of the Finnish and Soviet peoples. There stands on the magnificent waterfront of Helsinki a statue avowedly symbolising this relationship. It depicts an uneasily poised young woman, her attitude and features vividly expressive of the determined conciliation adopted when confronting a large and angry dog.

Cant colours most international attitudes – notably in the enthusiastic support for the Polish Solidarity movement expressed by Western leaders otherwise utterly opposed to trade union power – but the richest crop of cant is always reaped from the fertile soil of coercion. Neither those who exercise coercion nor those who yield care to acknowledge its brutal influence.

Consider the following quotations from two British Foreign Secretaries, each of whom subsequently acquired added credibility by elevation to the post of Prime Minister:

> Why then . . . is there a crisis of confidence in the United Nations? The answer is that for the first time since its foundation a number of countries have voted publicly and without shame in favour of the use of force to achieve national ends . . . the use of force by India against Goa.[2]   (Home, 1961)

> Guatemala appealed to the United Nations and declared that she was the victim of external aggression . . . Mr Dulles was opposed to the inscription of the item on the agenda . . . the effect of the Anglo French abstentions was equivalent to a vote against . . . I was not entirely happy about these proceedings . . . Yet . . . first priority must be given to the solidarity of the Anglo-American alliance.[3] (Eden, 1954)

At long last, two nations, members and loyal members of the
United Nations, have dared to assert that no moral law can be
enforced unless it is supported and sustained by physical power.[4]
(Home on Suez, 1956)

Circumstances, in international relations, do alter cases.

Results being more important than motives it is necessary to
scrutinise with a cynical eye claims that forcible intervention in foreign
countries (Afghanistan in 1979 or the Lebanon in more recent years)
was a disinterested response to the request of the local government.
Coercion is a factor of which events will sooner or later establish the
significance. Special relationship, collective security, the extended
right of self defence, 'pre-emptive defensive strike' (a recent and
notable contribution from the Caribbean), uniting for peace, alliance
solidarity, resistance to aggression, the socialist commonwealth,
national liberation are all euphemisms. Who? Whom? is the initial
consideration; the ability to apply appropriate force the test; the
terminal situation the only basis for ultimate judgment.[5] No action is
good if the result is bad.

The prediction of terminal situations is notoriously difficult. It is
thus tempting not merely to excuse mistakes, but actually to determine
choices, by reference to whatever slogan, supposedly based on
abstract principle, happens to be in fashion at the critical moment and
in the capital concerned. History, that 'register of the crimes, follies,
and misfortunes of mankind',[6] has recorded the consequences, not
least during the last thirty years.

Negotiation is not a true alternative to reliance on coercion, because
negotiators must usually take into account the existence of at least
implicit coercion when they strive to reach a compromise or to smooth
the path for compliance. The value of negotiation, which is very great,
is that its success so often ensures that coercion remains implicit. It
can prevent a resort to coercive diplomacy, ensure that threats are not
translated into overt acts, allow those who commit such acts to escape
the response of war. Whether discreetly conducted by the traditional
methods of diplomacy, or noisily in public debate or dangerously in
the drama of crisis-management, negotiation is an essential feature of
all disputes not terminated by unconditional surrender. Coercion in
all its forms depends on negotiation for its outcome. But the velvet
glove of diplomacy can neither grasp nor manipulate a dispute if there
is no hand within it, no element, however remote, implicit, non-
violent, of coercion. Even among allies, or in the European Economic

Community or the Universal Postal Union, there always lurks the idea
that refusing the request of another government may lead to the denial
of one's own aspiration. Bargaining is better than bullying, but in the
end there is always someone who has to pay. If the loser is not always
the weakest, that is because skilful diplomats can sometimes convey
an exaggerated impression of the coercive potential of their own
government.

International law, not as it exists but as it might, offers a more
plausible alternative to coercion. Its claims can not be rejected merely
on the philosophical grounds that all law codifies the rights of power,
must change with the balance of power and ultimately depends on
coercion for its authority. When the law of England diverges from its
power base, juries refuse to convict, the Official Solicitor makes a
farcical intervention, judgments are ignored or defied, the Director of
Public Prosecutions or the Attorney General becomes deaf or blind.
Nevertheless, even allowing for the fact that the powerful have easier
access to the courts and better prospects of success, many disputes are
resolved, not by any comparison of the coercive potential of the
parties, but through the application by an accepted tribunal of
generally agreed rules. It is by no means a perfect system, but its
extension to disputes between governments would at least reduce the
incidence of war, violence and coercive diplomacy.

It does not even matter that some governments would always
disregard an unfavourable judgment and that many would do so
whenever they considered their vital interests to be adversely affected.
Equal justice has nowhere been achieved, but many disputes would
never assume a coercive character and others would be peacefully
resolved if international law commanded even a fraction of the respect
accorded, in most civilised states, to domestic law. The real obstacle is
the absence of any general agreement on the rules of international law
or on the authority qualified to give them binding interpretation.

The author first experienced this problem at his first diplomatic
post. He was given the task of making representations to the Indonesian Ministry of Foreign Affairs in a very minor dispute. Instructions
from the Foreign Office to the Embassy said the legal position was
crystal clear, but he took the precaution of carrying with him the text-
book giving chapter and verse for the impregnability of the Foreign
Office view. Alas, the Indonesian official he encountered had open on
his desk another text-book, equally bulky, of similarly imposing
authorship and also published, at much the same date, in England.
This expressed, no less firmly, an opposite view. The experience was

repeated until the author was convinced, by advancing age, of the futility of such arguments.

Of course, they ought to be resolved by the International Court of Justice at The Hague. But many governments either altogether reject its jurisdiction or else accept it with major reservations. This tends to discourage resort to the Court even by more respectful governments. Such scant regard for the Court can not be ascribed only to bloody-minded nationalism or even to the fact that the Court's judgments are so often disregarded by the unsuccessful party. It also reflects fundamental disagreement on the content of international law.

In the Anglo-Icelandic fishing dispute, for instance, Iceland took no notice of the International Court's endorsement of the British case. As an ingenious Icelandic author has explained,[7] the Court was relying on principles of international law that were obsolete because they reflected the discredited colonialist system. In any case, Iceland could not be bound by any legal doctrines to which she had not expressly consented.

This is an awkward argument, particularly when one considers the obstacles which so long delayed the negotiation of the latest convention on the Law of the Sea and which still frustrate its ratification and entry into force. Nevertheless the Icelandic contention would be echoed by many other states. It is further complicated by the traditional disagreement concerning the validity of treaties. It would be wearisome to rehearse all the hypocritical arguments excited by this concept, but one deserves mention, both because it is now topical (though also ancient) and because it offers such a splendid example of the enduring and universal influence of cant. This is the contention that treaties need not be respected if they were originally negotiated on an 'unequal' basis (see Chapter 10 for examples). Any government conscious of irksome obligations and capable of organising a little historical research is likely to be attracted by this view. There may be, among the tens or even hundreds of thousands of treaties ever signed, a few that were negotiated on an entirely equal basis, without a shadow of even implicit coercion, but the examples do not spring readily to mind, least of all among those treaties which terminated conflicts or prevented the translation of threats into overt acts. Cardinal Alberoni was more candid and more accurately descriptive of enduring international realities when he declared, in 1717, 'it is a well known principle that princes and states are not bound to observe a treaty contrary to their interest'.[8]

The most, unfortunately, that can at present be said for

international law as an alternative to coercion is this. If two friendly states are involved in a dispute of no great importance to either, arguments based on such concepts of international law as they have in common will be seen as offering an alternative to arguments based on calculations of the coercive balance between them. In such situations the idea that international law exists does really assist the resolution, occasionally even the avoidance, of disputes. It is a pity that such disputes are neither the most frequent nor the most serious.

The United Nations, no less than its predecessor, the League of Nations, was originally envisaged by the optimistic as offering a more realistic approach to the peaceful resolution of disputes. Even in the absence of any general agreement on the rules of international law, even without a tribunal capable of delivering judgments that would command acceptance, even if law lacked coercive authority, surely a political consensus was possible. If enough governments, conscious of a common interest in peace and stability, joined in advocating a particular solution to some dispute, surely the parties concerned would accept the general verdict as a sensible compromise and renounce, however grudgingly, the use or threat of force to pursue their more extreme aspirations.

It does not often happen. The United Nations – the very name is cant – is a political organisation and its members are naturally guided by considerations of political advantage in casting their votes. The author was once required to solicit Lebanese support in the General Assembly for the British position on Gibraltar. He argued that international acceptance that geographical unity rather than the wishes of the inhabitants should determine the fate of the small neighbours of larger states might have disagreeable implications for Lebanese independence. The Lebanese official concerned (a Christian naturally) thought that an excellent point, but regretted that the Lebanon must vote with the rest of the Arab League. Now, if there was any chance of trading an Arab vote on Gibraltar for a British vote on the Palestine cause . . . .

That is the way majorities are achieved in the United Nations. Everybody does it and only the politically naive can call it discreditable. It is cant to ascribe to a majority in one's favour the moral force of world opinion, but to regard the opposite result as an unsavoury combination or as reflecting some 'double standard'. The verdicts of the United Nations are the vector sum of conflicting national interests and aspirations, many of them heavily influenced by relationships of implicit coercion. It is not only because these verdicts command no corporate power of coercion that they are so often disregarded. They also lack any claim to moral authority.

This does not mean that the existence of the United Nations organisation serves no useful purpose. It provides a forum in which the nations of the world, particularly those without widespread diplomatic representation or easy access to the media, can ventilate their grievances and their aspirations before a wider audience. Without the United Nations the views of many governments would be little known and even less heeded. The organisation is also the cosmetician of coercion. This can be encouraged (Korea or the Congo), condoned, excused, ignored or condemned – to the diplomatic (and sometimes the domestic) advantage of some governments and to the detriment of others. The United Nations usually provides a rough and ready indicator of the internationally perceived balance of implicit coercion.

It does not, unfortunately, always offer useful guidance to governments in dispute. The most overwhelming majorities contain few states prepared to back their votes with deeds, and enthusiasm is usually proportional to distance and detachment from the conflict. The classical example is the reaction of the League of Nations (often imitated by the United Nations) to Soviet invasion of Finland in 1939. Mannerheim's brief description can scarcely be bettered.

> While countries like Argentina, Uruguay and Colombia took an energetic stand for our country at the League of Nations 20th Assembly, one was forced to witness Sweden, Norway and Denmark declaring that they could not agree to any sanctions against the Soviet Union... the Scandinavian countries abstained from voting when the question of the aggressor being excluded from the League was being taken up.[9]

Mannerheim had little use for cant and saw no need to criticise this obvious response to the influence of implicit coercion.

At any given time, of course, there is always a slogan (the old word was 'cry') which is fashionable in the United Nations and which influences votes, as happens in the domestic politics of many nations, whenever the outcome does not particularly matter to those who cast them. In such cases there is no compelling reason why these votes should matter to anyone else.

In the real world there is no basis for choice that offers a satisfactory alternative to calculation of the coercive equation. This is a pity, because even those willing to attempt such calculations more often than not manage to get their sums wrong.

COERCIVE DIPLOMACY   I: DEFINITION

Against this background it is time to take a closer look at coercive diplomacy, not as a principle to be approved or condemned, but as a practice to be defined, described and analysed.

It has already been suggested that coercive diplomacy may be distinguished from ordinary diplomacy by its resort to direct threats or overt acts, but this distinction needs to be made more precise. The language employed by many governments in their routine exchanges could reasonably be called threatening without necessarily being coercive. Scarcely a month passes, for instance, without one Super Power telling the other that its conduct is increasing the likelihood of nuclear war. The threat is terrible but, even if constant repetition had not eroded any conviction it may once have carried, it is not specific. It is the modern equivalent of threatening one's adversaries with the wrath of God.

To be coercive a threat must be more than a generalised prediction of disastrous consequences, however plausible, in the indeterminate future. It must express readiness to do something injurious to the interest of another government unless that government either takes, or desists from or refrains from some indicated course of action. It must also constitute a clear departure from the established pattern of relations between the two governments concerned.

For instance, all the nuclear weapon states maintain missiles aimed at one another. From time to time they reiterate their determination to fire those missiles if they or, in some cases, their allies are attacked. This is a threat of the utmost gravity; it is specific, and it is sufficiently coercive to be described as a deterrent. But it is not coercive diplomacy, because it is not related to any particular dispute, but a standing feature of an established pattern of implicit coercion.

On the other hand, the news in October 1973 that US nuclear forces had been placed on the alert (DEFCON III) was coercive diplomacy (an overt act as well as a threat) because it was an exceptional measure clearly related to the US–Soviet dispute over the Arab–Israeli War and obviously meant to cause the Soviet Union to refrain from their apparent intention of sending troops to the Middle East. It was an unspoken but quite specific threat of war.

This is the most extreme form of coercive diplomacy, both because of its inherently dangerous character and because it comes so close to that uncertain boundary where diplomacy, even in the broadest sense of the word, ends and war begins.

This problem was discussed in an earlier work[10] and the distinction then attempted, however unsatisfactory, still seems to the author rather more helpful than rival formulations.

War is a violent conflict between states in which policy is determined by the desire to inflict injury rather than the hope of positive advantage. In peace, governments have to explain why they have injured foreigners; in war, why they have not. Coercive diplomacy, on the other hand, is intended to obtain some specific advantage from another state and forfeits its diplomatic character if it either contemplates the infliction of injury unrelated to obtaining that advantage or results in the victim attempting the infliction of injury after the original objective has been either achieved or abandoned. Coercive diplomacy is thus an alternative to war and, if it leads to war, we must not only hold that it has failed; we may even doubt whether it ever deserved the name.

An obvious case in point is the Argentine occupation of the Falkland Islands on 2 April 1982. As argued in Chapter 6 this was clearly neither meant nor expected to start a war. It was a classical instance of coercive diplomacy, the use of definitive force[11] to create a *fait accompli* in which the victim could only acquiesce. If it had succeeded, it would have settled a long-standing dispute in Argentina's favour. Because it led to war, it failed.

The threat or use of armed force, however, is only the dramatic tip of the iceberg of coercive diplomacy. Most applications are less sensational and, depending on the nature of the dispute and the relationship between the two countries concerned, often more effective. In 1954, for instance, the nature of the response required from the allies of the United States to the conflict in Indo-China became a matter of dispute between Britain and the United States. When Eden, then Foreign Secretary, told the House of Commons on 23 June 'I hope that we shall be able to agree to an international guarantee of any settlement that may emerge at Geneva . . . a reciprocal arrangement in which both sides take part, such as Locarno', this was deeply resented in the United States as a proposal to legitimise the rewards of conquest. On 30 June, therefore, the US House of Representatives resolved to withhold aid from governments committed by treaty to maintain Communist rule over any defined area in Asia.[12]

This was an exercise of coercive diplomacy because it was a specific threat to do something injurious to the interests of other governments unless they refrained from an indicated course of action in a particular dispute. It was an exceptional departure from the established pattern of international relations. It was also effective. No more was heard of the Locarno concept.

Whatever the method adopted, coercive diplomacy is normally exercised by one government against another. Many of the exceptions to this rule are more apparent than real. When Iranian students made hostages of American diplomats in Tehran or British commercial firms were, on various occasions, subjected to American sanctions, neither the Iranian nor the British Government remained a passive spectator of these events. Even if they had, the Iranian Government would still have been exercising coercion and the British suffering it. Governments can not renounce responsibility for their own nationals within their own state without losing their international credibility as a legitimate national authority.

Of course, many governments do forfeit this authority by their inability to control domestic dissidence. They may then acquiesce in, or even invite, foreign intervention against their own nationals. Arguments for or against the legitimacy of such a government are irrelevant: acquiescence in foreign intervention is an abdication of national authority. Such intervention, unless it leads to war, is always an act of coercive diplomacy, even if the apparent victim is a nation, or part of a nation, rather than a government.

Whatever may be said, either by the intervening government or by the government allegedly requesting assistance, injurious action against foreign nationals in their own state will always be generally perceived as undertaken in furtherance of the foreign policy of the intervening state. If it is not war, it can only be coercive diplomacy.

In the light of these arguments and examples the following definition may be suggested.

Coercive diplomacy is a resort to specific threats or to injurious actions, otherwise than as an act of war, in order to secure advantage, or to avert loss, in the furtherance of an international dispute or else against foreign nationals within the territory or the jurisdiction of their own state.

COERCIVE DIPLOMACY   II: METHODS

Coercive diplomacy may be attempted in one of four main modes. If it is to be *definitive*, the objective is the creation of a *fait accompli* which the victim can not resist and to which he can only respond by acquiescence or escalation. The presumption is that he will acquiesce. If it is to be *purposeful*, the objective is to threaten or inflict such damage that the victim will prefer to escape further pain by adopting the indicated course of action. If it is to be *catalytic*, the guiding principle is that raising the temperature will, even in the absence of coercive measures directly relevant to the dispute, encourage a disposition to compromise or compliance by the victim. If it is to be *expressive*, then it is more important to emphasise one's own attitude than to influence the conduct of the adversary, though this distinction is not always clearly apparent to the initiating government.[13]

In all these modes, coercive diplomacy may be attempted by a considerable variety of methods.

The most cost-effective are usually those which arise naturally from an established pattern of implicit coercion. For instance, in 1949 the United States Government, anxious to ensure that the Netherlands responded positively to Indonesian aspirations towards independence, temporarily suspended Marshall Plan aid to the Netherlands. This coercive act was effective because the Netherlands Government had already accepted a dependent relationship. It was psychologically more ready to yield to the turning of an admitted screw than a government which had not previously acknowledged dependence: Italy in 1935, for instance, or Rhodesia in 1969. It has been well argued that coercion is more dependent on the reactions of the victim than on the actions of the executant.

Decision-makers are creatures of habit. The withdrawal of an advantage sanctified by custom may well seem more terrible than the imposition of unfamiliar sanctions in an unprecedented environment. The withdrawal of what exists is clear and certain: what might happen in a hypothetical situation is, at best, hypothetical.

It would nevertheless be seriously misleading to suggest that any kind of coercive diplomacy, whatever the mode and even if the method arises directly from an established pattern of implicit coercion, enjoys an inherent prospect of success. So much depends on the nature and circumstances of the dispute, on the identity of the parties and on other factors that vary greatly from one case to another. In 1973, for instance, the Organisation of Petroleum Exporting Countries (OPEC) startled the world by the success of their coercive diplomacy. In the first flurry of alarm and excitement, the importers of primary products feared, and the producers hoped, that a new and generally applicable instrument of coercion had been dis-

covered. Many analysts, the author included, uneasily foresaw an era
of dispute, conflict and even war arising from mounting competition
for access to scarce resources.

Ten years later such dramatic predictions seem less plausible. Even
the initial success of OPEC was exaggerated at the time. Raising the
price of oil, admittedly, was a definitive act of coercive diplomacy
which worked. In spite of threatening noises from the United States it
commanded general acquiescence, however reluctant. Even if the
advantages to OPEC have been somewhat eroded by subsequent developments, many of them actually triggered by the initial success, the
oil producers are still benefiting from their coercive diplomacy.

The results of the employment, by Arab oil producers, of
production cuts and selective embargoes as a purposeful instrument of
coercive diplomacy are harder to analyse. At the time, of course, they
produced a degree of panic in importing countries, particularly those
of Western Europe. The shift in publicly expressed attitudes to the
Palestine dispute and the marked increase in European deference to
Arab susceptibilities have been lasting. A new relationship of implicit
coercion has been established, though this may perhaps be ascribed to
the impact of cuts in production and to the definitive increases in the
price of oil even more than to the purposeful use of embargoes. Arab
gains from this kind of coercive diplomacy may be contrasted with the
failure of terrorism, which attracted much initial publicity for the
Palestinian cause but, as counter-measures were adopted, probably
more diplomatic penalties than rewards.

Nevertheless, the oil embargoes were originally conceived as a
weapon against Israel. Without writing a history of the Middle East
during the last ten years it would be rash to assert that the position of
Israel was entirely unaffected by the embargoes, but it can certainly be
said that their practical results were unimpressive.

That, of course, was because the United States not only refused to
comply, but themselves resorted to coercive diplomacy by threatening
military intervention in the Middle East. How far these threats, which
aroused some alarm in European capitals, were responsible for the
withering away of the embargoes is uncertain. The destruction of
Israel commanded less widespread support among oil producers than
a higher price and was obviously more difficult to achieve. But it may
reasonably be argued that the threat of military intervention was more
efficacious than the reality would ever have been. That was generally
regarded at the time as a recipe for disaster, if not for general war.
Threatening intervention – by well-publicised military and naval

manoeuvres in 1974 – may thus be described as a catalytic use of coercive diplomacy.

A variety of expedients were employed for the expressive use of coercive diplomacy against the Soviet Union in response to events in Afghanistan and Poland and, more recently, the destruction of a Korean airliner. Neither the withdrawal of athletes from the Olympic Games, nor the cancellation of concerts, nor the temporary suspension of some commercial flights seems to have achieved anything but an outlet for emotion. Such measures (arguably less counter-productive than the more traditional practice of breaking embassy windows) will nevertheless continue to be attempted by governments attaching more importance to their own motives than to the results of their actions. The most ludicrous instance known to the author was the emergency telegram from the Foreign Office to the British Legation in Budapest at the height of the fighting following the Hungarian Revolution of 1956, prohibiting attendance at the Soviet Ambassador's National Day Party (which, of course, he never dreamed of holding on that particular 7th of November). But the expressive use of coercive diplomacy is usually cant in action: American gestures against the Soviet Union in the early eighties when contrasted with continuing sales of grain; the seizure by the British Customs in 1983 of Argentine books purchased by British university libraries after the grant, in the same year, of British credits to rescue Argentina from financial collapse.

COERCIVE DIPLOMACY   III: EFFICACY

Perhaps the most difficult problem confronting any student of coercive diplomacy is to discriminate between success and failure in its results. Any judgment is bound to be subjective and to depend on the uncertain answers to such questions as: what was the purpose of the initiating government; was it substantially achieved; was success lasting or transitory; did it lead to war or other undesirable consequences; was the result worth the cost of coercion?

It would be idle to pretend that any of these questions can be answered with a precision capable of commanding general agreement. Yet some attempt must be made to devise a rough and ready yardstick. Governments, after all, frequently resort to coercive diplomacy. If even they can not measure the results, the expedient will forfeit all claim to rationality and decision-makers will continue to be guided by motives of an emotional character rather than by any plausible prediction of the consequences of their actions. This would be regrettable.

The first obstacle is obvious. At what moment is it appropriate to invoke 'the unerring sentence of time'? Any kind of coercion not only has results: it has repercussions. These may extend over centuries – as with the fourteen sieges of Gibraltar – and constantly call in question the initial result. The battle of Culloden was exceptional in deciding, for a period now approaching two and a half centuries, English dominance of Scotland. There is always a temptation for historians commenting on contemporary events to emulate the legendary Chinaman, in the early years of this century, who considered it distinctly premature to describe the consequences of the French Revolution of 1789.

Such time-scales are irrelevant for decision-makers. The mainly elderly rulers of countries that are often politically unstable have a temporal horizon limited by their personal prospects of retaining power. Five years is nearer the maximum than the average.

That is not the only reason for suggesting a lapse of five years as the latest reasonable date for assessing the results of coercive diplomacy. Nowadays the evolution of international disputes is rapid. A dispute is exceptional if its nature, to say nothing of the surrounding framework of international relations and coercive balances, is recognisable after an interval of five years. If one wishes to argue about cause and effect, success or failure, one must do so soon. Otherwise the debate will be both academic and infinite.

Even within an arbitrary time-scale there is a further difficulty. Governments resorting to coercive diplomacy usually hope to improve what they regard as an unsatisfactory situation, but the degree of improvement aimed at or achieved is not always as obvious as it is in the 'before and after using' advertisements on television. Every kind of coercive diplomacy has been attempted, by numerous governments, during the last fifteen years, in relation to the continuing crisis in the Lebanon, but the situation in that country has never crystallised long enough to warrant any judgment that a particular foreign government had either succeeded or failed in its purpose. The same consideration applies to the remarkable variety of methods. It may safely be said that the USS NEW JERSEY had no definitive role to play, but, at the moment of writing, it is still too soon to describe her appearance off the coast in 1983 as either purposeful, or catalytic or expressive. Not only has the Lebanese problem been in constant evolution: so have the apparent objectives of other governments. The criteria, no less than the critical moment, for discriminating between success and failure have always been in dispute.

The results of coercive diplomacy, as of most human actions, are often uncertain, but this is not invariably the case. Sometimes success or failure, when measured within the arbitrary time-scale suggested and on the basis of the apparent objectives of the initiating government, seem clear enough. If there is a worse mistake than believing coercive diplomacy to be a reliable expedient, it is to assume that it never works.

In 1968, for instance, the purposeful use of limited force ensured the resumption by Czechoslovakia of her obedient role as a Soviet satellite. A clear success, even if it had lasted only five years instead of over fifteen. On the other hand, greater use of the same expedient has not so far reinforced Soviet ascendancy in Afghanistan. After nearly five years, a clear failure, even if it were to succeed in ten. It is highly improbable that the Soviet Union ever contemplated so long and arduous a struggle in 1979 – any more than the United States on their first, limited, intervention in Vietnam.

Definitive force, in 1976, allowed Israel to avoid being coerced by the plight of the hostages at Entebbe and scored a resounding success. When the same expedient was attempted in 1980 by the United States, in answer to the similar exploitation of hostages by Iran, it was a miserable failure and aggravated American humiliation.

In 1980 a purposeful use of coercive diplomacy enabled Britain to extract money from the European Economic Community by threatening to obstruct Community business. That was a success even if, in 1983, Britain had to threaten sharper measures in quest of further concessions. Similar tactics are often employed, with results that vary widely, by most members of the Community.

The riskier and more costly expedient chosen by members of the North Atlantic Alliance, from 1979 onwards, to secure a reduction in Soviet deployment of intermediate range missiles is harder to classify. If plans for a corresponding deployment of American missiles were seriously intended as a purposeful use of coercive diplomacy, they appear, as the five-year-limit approaches, to have failed. The Soviet leaders have consistently refused to sacrifice real missiles to escape the threat of a conjectural counterpart. There was, of course, a precedent for such an unequal bargain in the Washington Naval Treaty of 1922. This registered American success in a skilful employment of coercive diplomacy against Britain, who had ended the First World War as she began it – the world's strongest naval power. The United States

Government, however, threatened to embark on a huge programme of naval construction unless Britain reduced her existing navy to an agreed parity with the United States. Britain, lacking either the will or the resources for such a naval race, complied.

In 1979 and subsequent years, however, the position of the Soviet Union *vis à vis* the United States, to say nothing of Russian feelings of fear and hostility, was rather different from Britain's sixty years earlier. Coercive diplomacy does depend rather heavily, for its prospects of success, on the response to be expected from the victim. This is only one of the reasons why every resort to coercive diplomacy must be judged in the context of the particular dispute concerned.

Nobody, of course, expects much useful result from the expressive use of coercive diplomacy. The exclusion from the White House during the Nixon Presidency of representatives of governments openly opposed to American policy in Vietnam certainly mortified many foreign diplomats forced to fall back on the State Department, but was otherwise of questionable advantage to American policy. And Greek abstention from NATO naval exercises probably reinforced doubts about the value of Greece as an ally instead of attracting support for Greek disputes with Turkey.

The instances quoted earlier nevertheless suggest that it is frequently possible to discriminate between success and failure if the results of coercive diplomacy are examined at the appropriate moment and in the context of a particular dispute. The question that remains is whether such isolated treatment is permissible in view of the multiple interactions characteristic of all aspects of international relations. At first sight the events of 1973 offer strong support for a contrary view. The coercive diplomacy exercised by the United States against the Soviet Union has already been mentioned, but this was a response to Soviet threats of military intervention in the Arab–Israeli War. It has even been suggested that Egypt did not attack Israel in the hope of victory, but as an extreme exertion of catalytic coercive diplomacy, though this is an argument that smacks of later rationalisation. More to the point is that everyone concerned but not directly involved in the fighting resorted to coercive diplomacy: American pressure on Israel; the Arab oil embargo; the confrontation of the Sixth Fleet by the Soviet Mediterranean Squadron. Many more instances could be quoted and some of them ascribed to earlier events. For example, the denial to the United States by some of her European allies of facilities for the resupply of Israel may have been more than a purposeful or expressive response to the events of October. It could also have reflected some resentment of the coercive aspects of Kissinger's earlier Year of Europe, his unsuccessful efforts, also in 1973, at 'tightening the bonds of the Alliance'.[14] Is it reasonable to assess any one act of coercive diplomacy during 1973 in isolation from all the interlocking events of what might well be called The Year of Coercive Diplomacy?

It may seem unhistorical, but it makes some practical sense. Only the Almighty can discern all the multiple repercussions of a single act. Decision-makers are exceptionally diligent if they consider more than one dispute at a time or look even two or three moves ahead. Retrospective judgment of the results of coercive diplomacy may fairly be attempted on a short-term basis and in the context of a particular dispute, because that is how resort to this expedient is usually decided. Wider and remoter arguments are seldom so persuasive – either for or against.

So much would be gained, moreover, if decision-makers were to precede their resort to coercive diplomacy by a rigorous analysis of even the dispute to which it is directly relevant, that it seems unwise as well as impracticable to ask them to envisage the predicted terminal situation on a broader basis. There is some hope of guessing the practical results to be expected from the likely reactions of a limited number of actors in a brief period of time. When speculation is carried further, it tends to become so cloudy and so rich in alternative possibilities, that even the inherently fallible effort at rational prediction soon yields to argument by slogan and to decisions justified by their motives rather than by their expected results.

As an expedient for the resolution of international disputes coercive diplomacy occupies a position on the adversarial scale between the bland diplomacy of implicit coercion and the desperate brutality of war. It is the threat or use of limited force, even if that force need not be armed. The limitation imposed on the means should also apply to the scope of the dispute to be resolved, the nature of the end to be achieved, the reactions to be expected from the victim and to the time-scale of the entire operation. If the terminal situation desired demands the establishment or maintenance of an advantageous relationship that will be durable and wide-ranging, then reliance on the diplomacy of implicit coercion is obviously preferable. Occasionally, of course, a relationship based on implicit coercion may have to be maintained, or restored, by a sharp crack of the whip, as in Czechoslovakia in 1968. If this seems impossible and if neither compromise nor compliance can be considered, there may be no escape from war as the only means of either imposing or resisting a general and lasting settlement of disputes. War, however, is even more open-ended in its consequences than in its motives.

Coercive diplomacy is most efficacious when it removes the cause of dispute: freeing the Israeli hostages at Entebbe; recapturing the MAYAGUEZ off the Cambodian coast in 1975. It is still efficacious if it secures immediate advantage: preventing the airlift of Soviet troops into Egypt in 1973 or extracting British money from the European Community in 1980 – without removing the cause of dispute. It fails when there is no immediate advantage, or this is too dearly purchased, or there are early and damaging repercussions, or when coercive diplomacy leads to war. It also fails when no plausible comparison is possible between the initial objective and any terminal situation observable within five years. It is no more acceptable to argue that the consequences might have been even worse if nothing had been attempted, than it is to suggest that a favourable initial result was ultimately vitiated by wider or later repercussions or even by subsequent developments. Everything about coercive diplomacy is limited, not least the criteria for its success, Before, during and not long after, coercive diplomacy must be judged in the context of the particular dispute to which it is applied.

If the approach is switched from a retrospective diagnosis to an attempt at prognosis, the arguments advanced in Chapter 2 for regarding the efficacy of naval force as primarily dependent on the circumstances of particular disputes are readily extensible to all forms of coercive diplomacy. In international relations similar actions can not reliably be expected to have similar consequences: disputes are too different. Nevertheless it would obviously be desirable to attempt the formulation of some generalising principles, even if these went no further than a check-list of questions to be answered by decision-makers. This demanding task has not been attempted here. It is a responsibility that might well be assumed by the community of scholars concerned with international relations.

Unfortunately the idea of coercive diplomacy, let alone the reality, has a smell of brimstone distasteful to scholars. It has been studied, but usually in terms too abstract to be of much assistance to practitioners. This is a pity. Dangerous actions – and resort to coercive diplomacy is always dangerous – deserve more careful consideration than those expected to be innocuous. Regrettably, as explained in Chapter 11, there is a marked reluctance among scholars of international relations to admit the existence of any direct, causative or potentially beneficial connection between theory and practice. This reluctance is fully reciprocated by practitioners. As a result, coercive diplomacy tends to be exercised in a manner less rational, less systematic, less effective and – as a general rule – more harmful than might otherwise be the case. It would be extravagant to suggest that these deficiencies would be greatly alleviated, let alone eliminated, by providing practitioners with a better and more relevant theoretical grounding. Some slight improvement might, however, be attempted. It would at least deserve more respect than one widely prevalent academic attitude: 'I think it would be very wicked indeed to do anything to fit a boy for the modern world.'[15]

COERCIVE DIPLOMACY   IV: THE DARK SIDE

Ideally coercive diplomacy should only be attempted by those governments which, perceiving the consequences to themselves of a particular dispute as intolerable, are reasonably sure that a satisfactory terminal situation can be achieved either by action to remove the cause of dispute or else by action calculated to persuade another government or governments to adopt, refrain from or desist from some specific course of action.

These conditions are seldom achieved in practice. Governments, unlike those figments of the legal imagination, reasonable men, are not often guided in their choices by any clear conception of the predictable consequences of their actions. Their predominant concerns tend to be the present pain inflicted by foreigners, the domestic pressures to which this pain exposes them and the need for action, almost any action, to alleviate both pain and pressure.

Such mental processes are most nearly excusable when they result in an act of coercive diplomacy that is merely expressive. This seldom makes any positive contribution to resolving the dispute that excited such disagreeable emotions, but it sometimes provides a safety-valve for the escape of steam and prevents a more dangerous explosion. In 1967, for instance, the passions aroused among Lebanese Moslems by Israeli victories in the Six-Day War and by Nasser's lie that these had actually been achieved by British and American aircraft, caused the Lebanese President to expel the British and United States Ambassadors. This gesture, by a President who himself disclaimed any belief in the charges, did nothing to advance the Arab cause, but was arguably a necessary first step towards regaining control of Beirut from the mob recruited by the Egyptian Ambassador. It also enabled the President –

the Lebanon was then still just a state – to protect the two embassies with most of the few troops left in the capital. There were – the lapse of fifteen years has made this seem an almost idyllic result – no British casualties, if much damage to property.

There remain today so many states in which governmental ability to maintain law and order is tenuous that this kind of justification for the expressive use of coercive diplomacy still deserves consideration. Unfortunately it is often exploited by governments to excuse popular violence which they have themselves orchestrated.

That was the case in 1963, when the Chancery of the British Embassy in Jakarta, together with much other British property, was burned to the ground to demonstrate Indonesian hostility to the projected federation of Malaysia. The author, then serving in the South-East Asia Department of the Foreign Office, advocated the withdrawal of Embassy staff and the rupture of diplomatic relations as the appropriate expressive response. He was, it must be admitted, influenced by professional considerations: the general undesirability of acquiescing in organised violence against British diplomats. His superiors, including Lord Home, the Foreign Secretary, disagreed. No immediate advantage could be expected from the rupture of diplomatic relations, whereas some might yet be secured by their retention. It is hard to say who was right. The skeleton Embassy maintained in the servants' quarters of the Ambassador's residence did continue to provide information and an attenuated channel of communication during the years of Confrontation. On the other hand, would Confrontation have been so violent and so persistent without this initial and misleading indication of British docility? There is no certain answer, but one function of the expressive use of coercive diplomacy is undoubtedly to signal resolve. Indonesia did this more convincingly than Britain.

Curiously enough, the expressive use of coercive diplomacy is sometimes better attempted by actions than by words, by warships rather than by politicians or diplomats. Verbal threats, for instance, must often be pitched rather high, must even be inconveniently explicit, to carry much conviction. The days have long passed when a mere reference to 'an unfriendly act' would agitate the Chancelleries of Europe. The movements of warships, however, can still convey a sense of menace that is plausible to the victim because it is potent yet undefined, but convenient to the aggrieved government, because it is simultaneously impressive to domestic opinion and non-commital. Warships can always be withdrawn, provided the purpose of their movement has been left a little vague: verbal threats become embarrassing if they are neither productive nor implemented.

In 1983, for instance, the arrival of three Spanish warships in Algeciras Bay sufficiently demonstrated Spanish indignation at the visit to Gibraltar of a British squadron and Spanish determination to maintain their claim to the Rock. The protests and threats of the Spanish Foreign Ministry and the Spanish press were both excessive and unconvincing. When addressed to the presence on board a visiting ship of that junior officer, Prince Andrew, they introduced into the drama of the absurd an element of presumably unintended farce. Even this was less undignified than the King's earlier refusal to attend the Royal Wedding in London because the Prince and Princess of Wales would begin their honeymoon by joining the royal yacht at Gibraltar. An expressive act of coercive diplomacy that requires a King to visit political displeasure on a Princess does little to enhance respect for hereditary monarchy or to discharge the traditional royal function of setting standards of polite behaviour.

The danger of indulging one's own emotion is greatly increased when the outlet chosen is not confined to the expressive threat or use of force, but extends to actions of a definitive, purposeful or catalytic character. These always depend, for their success, on an accurate appreciation of the likely reactions of the victim. Can he be expected to acquiesce in a *fait accompli* or will he respond by escalating the dispute and, if so, with what consequences? Will the infliction of pain and damage cause him to make concessions and what kind of force is appropriate to this purpose? Will a catalytic threat or use of force, to raise the temperature of the crisis, make the dispute easier or harder to resolve? What, in fact, is the desired terminal situation and what kind of coercive diplomacy, if any, can be expected to achieve it?

These are all thoroughly difficult questions and the coolest heads do not always find the right answers. But, if the questions are not even asked, if cool has been lost, if the objective is emotional release and the motives of action seem more important than the expected results, then the prospects are poor indeed.

Gavrilo Princip, interrogated after he had killed the Archduke Franz Ferdinand von Österreich Este and his wife, Sophie Duchess of Hohenberg, at Sarajevo on 28 June 1914, explained: 'My thought was therefore only on the success of the assassination; of some unfavourable consequence or other I had not thought at all.'[16]

Such attitudes are censurable even in youthful fanatics; they are almost incomprehensible in responsible statesmen.

Unfortunately they occur. Instant retaliation – the favourite retort of the Israeli Government, for instance, to terrorist attacks – is perhaps the most understandable. It is a human reaction to hit back at once, without even thinking about it, to let instinct trigger a reflex. It seldom does much good unless the assailant can be identified, located and incapacitated.

Matters are not much improved by deferring retaliation until plans have been elaborated and preparations completed, if the objective is still emotional satisfaction and not the attainment of a predictably advantageous terminal situation. Delay did Eden no good in the Suez crisis of 1956, because he used the interval to elaborate justifications for his motives, not to analyse the likely consequences of his actions.

The prognosis is equally poor when emotional outrage becomes a pretext for purposes which can not be subjected to critical examination, because they can not be openly admitted: eliminating the threat posed by Slav minorities to the internal stability of the Austro-Hungarian Empire in 1914; or rescuing the Saigon Government by crushing North Vietnam after the ambiguous incidents in the Gulf of Tonkin in 1964. The disastrous consequences of those two decisions must be expected by anyone who closes his eyes before pulling the trigger.

Coercion, however coolly calculated, is always risky, but the risks are greater when it is prompted by emotion or has to be justified by emotional considerations. Bernard Shaw once argued that children should never be struck except in anger. This is not true of nations.

One reason why the angry use of coercive diplomacy is nevertheless so often attempted is that an emotional resort to force frequently attracts popular support. Not only is it consistent with unthinking human impulse, but it conforms to the patterns of behaviour which popular culture depicts as admirable. The heroes of fiction, in print, on stage or big or little screen, are much given to righteous indignation. If they are impulsive and hot-tempered, these are seen as the characteristics of a warm-hearted and generous temperament. Villains are cold and calculating, much inclined to prefer legal or political stratagems to the heroic use of fist or gun and ready to fight only when circumstances give them an unfair advantage. Soldiers and men of action are usually heroic figures: lawyers, diplomats and negotiators are not.

Chapter 12 considers one important branch of popular culture – the thriller – and emphasises the political importance of one of its fundamental postulates: the menace that can only be met by force, the wrong for which society provides no legal remedy. In the dozen years since that was written, popular fiction has increasingly emphasised the heroic aspects of the use of force and, whether coincidentally or otherwise, these have become more prominent in popular reactions to events in the real world. Arming the police, for instance, long regarded in Britain as the desperate expedient of lesser breeds without the law, is now generally accepted as a frequent necessity. The violent rescue of hostages from the Iranian Embassy in London by soldiers of the SAS Regiment in 1980 was not only nationally popular, but attracted foreign applause. Of course, it may be said that such developments, in Britain as in many other countries, are no more than an inevitable response by the state to the increasing violence of its enemies, criminal or political. Chicken and egg arguments are better avoided. It is enough to note that the use of violence, political attitudes to it and the assumptions of popular fiction have all evolved in step.

This evolution has not been confined to domestic politics. It is hard to think of any international event during the last decade which excited such admiration and applause in so many countries, as the daring, but violent and illegal, rescue of Israeli hostages from Entebbe Airport in 1976. Its impact was far greater than that of the Final Act of the Conference on Security and Cooperation in Europe signed at Helsinki in 1975. The dramatisation of Entebbe provided rich rewards for the producers of competing paper-backs, films and television programmes: Helsinki was the stuff of text-books.

Where faction has led, fiction has not been far behind. Frederick Forsyth's able and successful thriller, *The Devil's Alternative*,[17] takes coercive diplomacy for its subject and depicts its employment by and against many governments, in various ways and for different purposes. Naturally coercive diplomacy is most attractively presented when its victims are malignant conspirators in the Politburo, but even Soviet use of this technique is allowed to seem both necessary and admirable and, in the end, the peace of the world is preserved and massive environmental pollution avoided by East–West connivance in expedient murder. The book is not alone in equating the heroic qualities of political leaders with their readiness to resort to the threat or use of force, but its distinguishing feature is the skill and sophistication of its depiction of coercive diplomacy as a valid and even indispensable alternative to war.

If real leaders were as cool, as rational and as fundamentally cautious as those portrayed in this book, its message might be considered salutary. As things are, the fictional triumphs of coercive diplomacy are too easy, too generally beneficial and, above all, too glamorous to make this excellent book desirable bedside reading either for political leaders or their electorates.

As for lesser, shriller, more one-sided writers, whether avowedly of fiction or ostensibly of reportage and commentary, their impact on the climate of opinion is seldom conducive to the sober analysis of terminal situations. It found expression in a Californian comment on the invasion of Grenada in October 1983: 'Thank God, we finally have a real man in the White House.'

ENDS, MEANS AND MOTIVES

These considerations concerning coercion, compromise and compliance have been heavily dependent on a much criticised approach to the analysis of international relations: the assumption that decision-makers are rational actors capable of pursuing rational advantage if only they could correctly perceive the nature of the most advantageous result likely to be attainable and the right method of achieving it.

The objections to this assumption are as numerous as they are formidable. The powers of judgment of those who take decisions are frequently impaired by mental instability, physical disease or the trauma of domestic crisis. They may actually be so incapacitated that decisions are taken in their name, but without their knowledge or that of the people they are supposed to lead (President Woodrow Wilson, for instance, or Sir Winston Churchill for a shorter period after his stroke). Moreover, even at the height of their powers, leading statesmen often reveal, to those who know them well, a disturbingly unconventional personality and temperament. Few British Prime Ministers, for instance, would have met the stringent requirements, based on thorough analysis of educational record, early career, family life, resistance to ordinary temptations, that establish the reliability, emotional stability and general worthiness of candidates for senior, but still distinctly subordinate, positions in any political, bureaucratic, commercial or military hierarchy. Leaders often have unusual characteristics.

Even if the actual decision-maker, whoever he may be, meets conventional standards of sanity, health, intelligence, industry and balanced judgment, who can be sure of his motives or of the impact of the extraneous pressures to which he may be subjected? Was President

Nixon, during the Watergate crisis, not only able to apply a dispassionate judgment to the important international issues which confronted him, but also actuated solely by considerations of the national interest of the United States?

These are difficult questions to which much argument has been devoted. So it has to a more fundamental problem: does the national interest really exist? Is it more than an euphemistic description of the resultant of conflict among the ruling class to promote different aspirations and assumptions? Does it make any sense at all to say that Ruritania has interests, aspirations, a policy or that Ruritanian decisions reflect anything but the outcome of an obscure power struggle among Ruritanian leaders, Ruritanian bureaucracy and, ultimately but rather vaguely, Ruritanian society?

This is not the place, in the final pages of an essay on a more restricted theme, to argue such fundamental issues. It may well be admitted that those who enjoy power, essentially the ability to make effective choices, want, more than anything else in the world, to go on enjoying power. It can also be agreed that many of the conditions for enjoying power have little to do with considerations of the national interest. Nevertheless, anyone who enjoys the power of leading a nation-state can not help realising that his enjoyment depends on the survival and independence of that state. National leaders, unlike dentists, doctors, physicists and ballet-dancers, can seldom expect a satisfactory alternative career either abroad or under foreign rule. Professionally, they are more committed to their own country than many other members of the privileged and successful class.

In time of crisis, whether external or internal, they may be slow to admit the existence of a choice between their own retention of power and the interests of the nation they lead, slower still to decide in favour of the latter. Such dilemmas are the exception rather than the rule. Of course, all decision-makers exaggerate their indispensability, the support they enjoy and their own mental and physical capacities. As a rule, however, they are at least sincere in regarding their own retention of power as compatible with the interests of their own nation-state.

It may be a very rough rule of thumb to regard national governments as seeking the interest of the nations they lead, but it is not obvious that any other working assumption would be of much practical assistance to anyone but partisans and historians. The latter can always rely on the unerring sentence of time, but this is a verdict for which decision-makers can seldom afford to wait.

Nor can students of international relations, who are not primarily historians, though they are foolish if they neglect the lessons of history. The study of international relations, as argued in Chapter 11, is an useful art or it is nothing at all. International relations is neither a science nor a pure subject. Its purpose, its utility and its justification depend on the ability of scholars to offer theoretical concepts which will assist practitioners in identifying the choices that confront them.

Much historical analysis of previous crises has rightly been concerned with the severe constraints on choice perceived by decision-makers at the time. These were not only the result of the personal and domestic pressures earlier mentioned, but often reflected sheer inability to understand foreign attitudes or the significance of external events. A determinist view of history, even the pessimistic conclusion that decision-makers are inevitably overwhelmed by the events they seek to control, is not only intellectually attractive, but may ultimately be judged, perhaps by historians in New Zealand, to have been correct.

It is nevertheless an attitude impermissible to the constructive student of international relations. He must continue, even in defiance of the historical evidence, to hope that his efforts may, ultimately and indirectly, impart an added tinge of rationality to the practical conduct of international relations. If he does so hope, he is presumptuous, perhaps foolishly optimistic, even naive. But what is the alternative? It is the assumption that no rational argument will ever influence practical decisions. That is the sin of despair and anyone who takes that view would do better to abandon international relations for some more rewarding subject: eschatology, for instance, the study of the Four Last Things.

All the evidence suggests that decision-makers are often either themselves irrational or else hopelessly constrained by irrational considerations. Nevertheless, it is necessary to assume the possibility of an exceptional state of affairs and to devise arguments addressed to that unlikely contingency. Otherwise there is no hope at all. Moreover, it did happen at least once: in the Cuban Missile crisis of 1962.

Even in the best of imaginable circumstances, however, no alternative policy, concept or assumption will receive any consideration unless it takes full account of the real world as it actually exists. In that world international relations are dominated by the trinity, perhaps the unholy trinity, of coercion, compromise and compliance. If attention, in this essay, has been focussed upon coercion, whether express or implicit, that has been because coercion is the active principle in international relations. Compromise and compliance are reactions or responses. Only results can decide the merits of any expedient, but the results of coercion might be less harmful, and bear more resemblance to intentions, if the process were better understood. Even poisons deserve more careful analysis than placebos.

2 The Diffusion of Maritime Power

Power does not exist. Not in any absolute sense. It is the ability to apply appropriate force about a given point.

Though true of any kind of power – thermonuclear fusion will not propel so much as a vacuum cleaner – this is an axiom which has often proved politically indigestible. Academics have been no less inclined than rulers to measure power by the aggregation of resources and to expect that power to be reflected in the attainment of political objectives. The frequent disappointment of such expectations has been attributed, as usually happens with unsound theories, to errors in observation, mensuration, calculation. Much effort has accordingly been devoted to refining and elaborating the criteria of power: not just the obvious economic, technological, military, demographic constituents, but such less tangible factors as political organisation, morale or motivation. The purpose has been to produce a definition of power that would not only be comprehensive, but would offer a reliable basis for comparing the power of one state with that of another. A recent study of the more limited subject of maritime power identified no less than thirty-nine constituent elements.

It would be wrong to describe these efforts as wasted. They dredged up much that was interesting and a little that was valuable. But they did not answer the essential question confronting every student of power.

Power to do what?

It is a terrible question. It opens an entire Pandora's box. Lenin's famous Who? Whom?'is only the first to emerge. There is When? and Why? and Where? Political considerations, geographical limitations, the exigencies of time, climatic factors buzz distractingly about the ears of decision-makers. The power accumulated, with effort and foresight, for one scenario proves irrelevant to another.

In 1917 the world's strongest battle fleet offered Britain no escape from the imminent prospect of decisive defeat in the U-boat war. In

36

1980 the United States, by any conventional measure a Super Power, were as deeply humiliated by the Iranians as, in 1968, they had been by the North Koreans. Power to do what?

There is no single answer to that question. One was once thought to exist for maritime power: command of the sea, the advantage from which all else flowed. Even in its palmiest days this was a concept exposed to numerous qualifications and exceptions. The appropriate force it permitted could, for instance, only be exercised against those who were vulnerable at sea or from the sea. That was why Bismarck could afford to declare his intention of sending for the police if the British fleet appeared off the coast of Pomerania during the Schleswig–Holstein crisis. The extent of this vulnerability has, moreover, greatly diminished with the improvement of terrestrial communications and of the political organisation of coastal states. The changes in what command of the sea can do are nevertheless less fundamental than the new obstacles to its creation.

A century ago a fleet at sea was safe from anything but a stronger fleet. Insofar, therefore, as command of the sea provided a force appropriate to the objective, that force could be an almost direct function of naval power. Command of the sea and all the benefits of that command were the predestined reward of a sufficiently superior fleet. Mines, torpedoes, aircraft, submarines and missiles have changed all that. In the words of Admiral Turner: 'it is no longer conceivable, except in the most limited sense, to totally control the seas for one's own use or to totally deny them to an enemy'. The most he thought the United States Navy could hope for was 'realistic control in limited areas and for limited periods of time'.[1]

Nowadays force can be used on, over or under the sea to protect or to deny a particular use of the sea. If even the United States can do so only 'in limited areas and for limited periods of time', it is clearly important to specify the use of the sea in question and the nature of the dispute. Both could vary enormously, as could the kind of force that might be appropriate. If we want to measure maritime power, there are as many yardsticks as there are different disputes.

In the first thirty-six years after the end of the Second World War, for instance, the Royal Navy were defeated by two countries: Albania, who inflicted severe damage and casualties on two British destroyers in 1946, and Iceland, whose gunboats successfully asserted her successive claims to exclusive fishing rights. No conceivable method of calculating resources could have supported the proposition that either possessed a maritime power remotely comparable to Britain's, yet each proved able, in the special circumstances of a particular dispute, to make more effective use of appropriate force.

Some disputes (though these were not among them) are so idiosyncratic that the kind of force appropriate to their resolution is unpredictable. In others appropriate force is available, but misapplied. Admiral Nagumo, for instance, did not have to lose the battle of Midway. Nobody can be sure of always being able to apply appropriate force in every dispute – let alone that success will result. Nevertheless, most countries do have a rough idea of the kind of disputes in which they might be involved. Some of these are manifestly beyond their capacities. If these contingencies are not altogether disregarded, then any plans must envisage other expedients than the application of appropriate force: alliance, neutrality, compromise, capitulation or, in some cases, deterrence. Even these, of course, may require readiness to employ some kind of force. There remain, for most countries, certain classes of potential dispute in which, against particular opponents and in favourable circumstances, advantage might be obtained or loss averted by the use of appropriate force.

About 113 countries maintain navies of one kind or another, though the *Military Balance* (the source of this figure) casts some doubt on the estimate by omitting all mention of Iceland.[2] A few of these navies are little more than harbour police; others are mainly intended to provide employment for the officer class. At least eighty of them, however, are meant to be capable of using force in some circumstances. The conditions could be rather restrictive: only in territorial waters; not beyond the 200-mile zone; not in the face of armed opposition; only against certain opponents; in low-level conflict only. But each of these navies has some kind of mission.

Now the conventional method of measuring maritime power, once the analyst gets beyond the mere counting of ships, has been to compare the magnitude and the variety of the different missions which various countries are regarded as capable of undertaking. American Secretaries of Defence, for instance, have spoken of the ability to fight 2½ or 1½ wars; the French Government once claimed for their navy 'un caractère polyvalent – pour toute mission';[3] navies are often classified as 'ocean-going' or 'coastal defence'. This kind of taxonomy is useful for many purposes and some indication of its requirements will be given at a later stage of the argument. But it does not meet the need for a functional definition of maritime power.

International relations, after all, is not league football. States are not required to fight one another in standard conditions and by uniform rules. A particular navy may be obviously incapable of nuclear war, total war, war with a Super Power, sustained combat with the navies of many other countries or any kind of distant operations. None of these deficiencies need deprive the state possessing that navy of a claim to enjoy significant maritime power. The test depends on the purposes for which power is required, on the kind of force that power is intended to produce and on the circumstances in which the application of force is contemplated.

For instance, long before there was any international acceptance of exclusive economic zones, the Ecuadorean Navy successfully arrested American vessels fishing on the high seas within 200 miles of the Ecuadorean coast.[4] For that purpose, therefore, Ecuador had maritime power. Admittedly this power could not have been exercised if political factors had not made it possible, but no political considerations would have stopped American fishing in the absence of Ecuadorean warships. Both considerations applied in 1977 when the Argentine Navy not only arrested nine Soviet and Bulgarian trawlers on the high seas, but fired on them and caused casualties.[5]

Naturally the ace of appropriate force is sometimes liable to be trumped by superior force. The former permitted Argentina in April 1982 to acquire the Falkland Islands. It must have been a most disagreeable surprise when Britain employed superior force to regain islands she had been unwilling to defend. The precedent of British passivity in the face of the 1974 Turkish invasion of Cyprus had surely encouraged quite different expectations in Buenos Aires. Error, unfortunately, is as endemic among politicians as admirals, as common in nominal peace as in outright war. If the ability to command success constituted an essential attribute of power, everybody could be reckoned impotent. Maritime power is no more than a plausible capability to employ force at sea for purposes regarded as nationally important. The value, absolute or relative, of that power is more dependent on the ability to match the particular requirements, in terms of appropriate force, of a given dispute than it is upon quantitative comparisons.

During the Vietnam War, for instance, one American analyst embarked on an elaborate calculation of the energy resources needed to deliver a specified volume of fire-power in the front line. He argued that the superiority of American resources so greatly outweighed the disadvantages of distance that the United States would always be able to apply superior force. Some factors, admittedly, were absent from his equation – not least the bicycles of Dien Bien Phu – but this was the wrong approach. What counts is a force appropriate to the dispute.

Five factors help to determine what is appropriate at sea: the location of the conflict; the constraints of time; the identity and motivation of the contestants; the international environment; and the level of conflict. They deserve separate consideration.

LOCATION OF THE CONFLICT

This is a factor of the utmost importance. The force required by either side tends to be directly proportional to the distance between the base and the scene of action; the force available to be inversely proportional.

Both propositions were well illustrated by the Falklands crisis, but they have important consequences for the whole concept of maritime power. A navy operating at a distance not only needs more ships to deploy even an equal force, but special kinds of ship: ocean-going warships, aircraft carriers, a fleet train. The navy operating in its own waters, on the other hand, may be able to make effective use of much cheaper vessels – missile-firing patrol craft or coastal submarines – whose lack of sea-keeping qualities is no impediment close off shore. They can be supported by land-based aircraft, even by coastal artillery or missiles. Mining is also easier for the coastal state. Last, but emphatically not least, a state conducting a conflict in its own waters can commit all its forces; the distant state must almost always withhold some for home defence.

Distance can thus be an equaliser in the balance of maritime power, which can not be measured or compared without regard to the location of the conflict. It also helps to determine the diffusion of maritime power. At a rough estimate and subject to other factors still to be considered, this is enjoyed by: in territorial waters – 75 states; in the adjacent sea – 25; up to a few hundred miles – 12; at greater distances – 4. Diffusion, in fact, diminishes with distance, because this restricts the ability to apply appropriate force.

THE CONSTRAINTS OF TIME

These are often, but not invariably, related to distance. They are of two kinds. The nature of the dispute may require the application of force to be immediate if it is to be effective, let alone appropriate. The classical example is the seizure of the USS PUEBLO by North Korean patrol craft in January 1968, when American deployment of a fleet that included 3 aircraft carriers merely emphasised the impotence of the belated.[6] British failure to intercept the German invasion fleet proved equally irretrievable in the Norwegian campaign of 1940. These were errors of judgment and, although the obstacles to timely naval intervention do increase with distance, readiness for action may be indispensable for the exercise of appropriate force even in coastal waters and thus an essential component of maritime power.

The second kind of constraint is the time for which conflict can be sustained, threatened or deterred. Here again distance is significant, but not necessarily decisive. The Soviet Navy maintained a more or less continuous presence off the coast of Guinea from 1971 to 1976.[7] Nevertheless, the accepted formula for naval operations that are both protracted and distant is three ships committed for every one engaged. Coastal states enjoy a much easier ratio.

To some extent time shares the equalising characteristics of distance, but in a less predictable manner. The advantages of promptness and endurance are more dependent on correct decisions than on inherent attributes, but, insofar as the latter are significant, the most important is redundancy: having resources not pre-empted by other tasks. The time-factor favours those nations which can keep forces at instant readiness, either in the expectation of dispute or in its prosecution. This gives the edge to the single-minded, who have only one use for their forces, and to the Super Powers, who have enough to spare for many purposes. Distance produced a pyramid in the diffusion of maritime power: a wide base of local effectiveness tapering to a narrow peak of universal competence. Time suggests an hourglass pattern: the committed bulging out the bottom and the Super Powers the top, those in the middle squeezed between their preoccupations and their capacity. The low-level Icelandic confrontation or the entirely non-violent Beira Patrol imposed a greater strain on the Royal Navy than would have been felt either by a coastal state operating in its own waters or by a Super Power. The equaliser is the fallible and unpredictable instrument of political judgment.

IDENTITY AND MOTIVATION

The identity of the contestants is obviously crucial for each of the five factors under consideration, but is not in itself decisive. The ability of any given state to apply appropriate force at sea varies very greatly with the circumstances of the dispute. One of these circumstances, of course, is the identity of the other party. The advantages enjoyed by the coastal state when conflict takes place in its own waters will be greater if the adversary is some distant country rather than a neighbour almost equally favoured by distance and time. But, even between the same pair of countries, the balance can vary. Iceland's ability to conduct a fishery dispute would have been much diminished if the scene had been the English Channel or the level of conflict higher. It has even been plausibly argued that the Falklands War might have had a different outcome if the distance of the Argentine airfields from the islands had been a hundred miles less. The identity of the contestants offers a clue, but not the solution, to their relative ability to apply appropriate force at sea.

Motivation is more important. Even at quite high levels of conflict it is both politically and militarily advantageous to be single-minded, particularly if this concentration on a single objective extends from the leadership to the people. Finland survived the Winter War, Britain escaped invasion in 1940, Vietnam defeated the United States because their enemies were less single-minded: they had conflicting priorities. Politically the case is obvious: the single-minded are ready to make more sacrifices, run greater risks, endure longer. Concentration of purpose can, however, also be a military equaliser, enabling one side to employ and hazard the whole of its forces, while the opponent must keep some back for other tasks and may be more reluctant to risk losses. Unequal motivation may also deprive the stronger side of the natural trump of escalation.

Small countries are not always more single-minded about the disputes in which they engage, but they are certainly less likely to be distracted by other enemies, by the susceptibilities of allies or by the complex web of inter-locking interests and commitments natural to great powers. Because small countries have fewer preoccupations, they also have a better chance to foresee, even prepare for, the few disputes in which they are ever likely to engage. Monomania may be exasperating to others, but it is a state of mind conducive to the deployment of appropriate force.

THE INTERNATIONAL ENVIRONMENT

The nature of the international environment and its influence on what constitutes appropriate force is a subject too vast and complex for brief discussion. A few very general propositions will have to suffice.

The first is that the international environment exercises a variety of constraints upon the application of any kind of force. The most important are military: the application of force may attract counter-measures by third parties (as when the United States resupplied Israel or the Soviet Union Vietnam); it may leave the user vulnerable to other enemies (as when a British naval concentration against Italy left only 1 cruiser, 17 destroyers and 9 submarines in home waters in March 1936 – when Germany occupied the Rhineland);[8] it may put at risk ships, bases or alliances needed for other purposes (as the Icelandic fisheries dispute hazarded the NATO base at Keflavik). There are also economic and diplomatic constraints: customers or creditors may be alienated; friends, patrons or influence lost. Censure by the United Nations, by foreign governments or by the media may not have much intrinsic significance, but it can sometimes adversely affect domestic support.

The second is that the incidence and importance of these constraints is extremely uneven. Some states and some uses of force are more exposed to international constraints than others. Attempts to explain this phenomenon are usually coloured by the political preconceptions of their authors and are too many and various for rehearsal here. Some obvious points, however, may be noted, with the reservation that each of them is subject to numerous exceptions in particular cases.

Sensitivity to international constraints tends to be proportional to the international involvement of the state concerned. As a general rule, therefore, constraints are more keenly felt by large, widely committed states than by small, self-contained neutrals. The allegedly greater vulnerability to international constraints of democratic states is a debatable point.

Constraints have more impact on the protracted use of force than on its swift exercise to create a *fait accompli*. On the clock of international awareness the sweep hand tends to react to any decisive event by returning to zero and starting again.

On the other hand, the effectiveness of international constraints tends to diminish as the level of conflict rises. If enough people are being killed, domestic opinion may disregard the views of those not at risk.

The countries least liable to international constraints are the single-minded: only those already in doubt heed the views of outsiders.

The international environment is thus much less regular, uniform or predictable as a factor influencing the nature of appropriate force than are distance, time, identity or motivation. In some disputes, however, it can be of great importance. In the Suez crisis of 1956, for instance, it was this factor, together with inadequate British motivation, that made Britain's naval force inappropriate and caused estimates of her maritime power to be revised downwards. Because of its somewhat random impact, it is the joker in the diffusion of maritime power, but it has some tendency to reinforce the equalising effects of other factors.

THE LEVEL OF CONFLICT

When it comes to equalisation, the level of conflict is a factor that cuts both ways. If it can be kept low enough, this favours small states, who can rely on obstruction, harassment, ramming and other expedients that cause few casualties but to which costly and sophisticated warships may find it difficult to respond without raising the level of violence. In such circumstances armed forces can be supplemented, or even replaced, by police launches, customs enforcement vessels or entirely civilian craft: tugs, fishing boats, yachts. Trawlers have often gathered to block the entrance to a port and might be able to close a strait. Greenpeace vessels have obstructed whaling, and other protest groups, with or without the encouragement and support of their national government, could interfere with dumping at sea or disputed exploration or exploitation of the sea-bed.

Icelandic conduct of the fisheries dispute with Britain is a classic case, but much of the French Navy had to be deployed to establish a maritime cordon around the controversial nuclear tests on the island of Mururoa. These were notable exceptions to the general rule that low-level conflict occurs primarily in coastal waters. Icelandic gunboats sometimes chased British trawlers for hundreds of miles.

Existing and likely developments in marine technology and the law of the sea are obviously increasing the scope for the kind of maritime dispute which confronts opposing political interests and aspirations without necessarily engaging national passions. Low-level conflict at sea must accordingly be regarded as probable and the use of appropriate force will be easier for the adjacent, for the ready, for those not under time pressure, for the single-minded, for those least exposed to international constraints. The lower the level of the ensuing conflict can be kept, the wider we must consider the diffusion of maritime power to be.

Low-level conflict is not, however, an option generally available. It exists only insofar as it is tolerated by those contestants capable of escalation. In some disputes, admittedly, escalation would be irrelevant. The United States could have devastated North Korea or Iran without thereby rescuing a single hostage. But Britain could have secured her fishing rights by attacking Iceland itself or merely by destroying Icelandic gunboats and fishing vessels. The Falklands crisis involved far more violence than Argentina can ever have contemplated when launching an operation intended to produce a bloodless *fait accompli*. The ace of appropriate force can be trumped.

This is where aggregate resources become important. There are four ways in which they can be employed, other factors permitting, to raise the level of a conflict. This can be made more sophisticated or more violent. The forces engaged can be increased or the scope of the conflict extended.

Turning the screw of sophistication can take many forms, for there is a wide variety of technological expedients which may be appropriate, yet available only to one side. American mining of the approaches to Haiphong in 1972 was a particularly interesting application of technological superiority, because it involved no increase in violence. This would not be the case if resort was had to missiles of longer range (used as early as 1967 to sink the Israeli destroyer EILAT). In some disputes electronic interference might be significant on its own, but in most cases technical wizardry would be employed to enhance the impact of weapons. Occasionally, in the Falklands conflict, for instance, one or two sophisticated ships, such as nuclear-propelled submarines, might exercise a disproportionate influence. Nevertheless, there will be few conflicts in which mere sophistication will alone be decisive. There are too many other factors to be taken into account.

One of them is the level of violence. It is only occasionally that it is possible to raise the technological level of conflict without also increasing its violence. 'Over-the-horizon' missiles, for instance, can be used to sink ships without fear of retaliation, but not to fire a shot across the bows. The presence of British nuclear submarines would probably not have kept the Argentine surface fleet in home waters if CONQUEROR had not sunk GENERAL BELGRANO. A higher level of violence may, of course, seem positively attractive to a contestant enjoying a clear advantage in the ability to employ it, but this expedient is likely to carry penalties in the international environment. Moreover, its effectiveness against a single-minded opponent is easily exaggerated. It is a trump, but not an infallible trump.

Escape is sometimes sought from this dilemma by mere expansion of the forces deployed, whether to over-awe the opponent or to execute some operation, such as blockade, requiring numbers rather than violence. The American naval blockade of Cuba during the 1962 Missile crisis or the demonstrative reinforcements of the Sixth Fleet on various occasions are examples. Unfortunately this form of escalation is inherently unstable. A superior fleet inevitably includes ships of high value which may be vulnerable to a single-minded opponent prepared to take the initiative in raising the level of violence. Both sides thus have cause to be quick on the trigger, as was shown in August 1981, when two Libyan aircraft were shot down by patrols from the USS NIMITZ.

Whatever the method adopted, therefore, the risk always exists that raising the level of conflict will also mean raising the level of violence. Escalation is thus an option of which the availability is not necessarily proportionate to aggregate resources. Admittedly the country with the most numerous and sophisticated weapons is physically capable of raising the conflict to a level at which the opponent can no longer compete. Political factors, however, may do much to equalise the ceilings of the two sides, if one of them happens to be noticeably less single-minded, more averse to violence and more exposed to international constraints. The capability for mere violence is also fairly widespread. Given the proliferation of modern missiles there are thirty or forty countries able to emulate Argentina and sink a British warship. At that level, if conflict is to continue, one or both sides are liable to seek or threaten the destruction of the opposing forces.

This can introduce a form of escalation that both sides may initially have wished to avoid: the extension of the conflict. The dispute over the Falkland Islands provided an example of partial and probably reluctant escalation. Argentina doubtless intended no more than a political application of limited naval force to create a localised *fait accompli* in which the adversary, being incapable of resistance at the scene of action, would have no option but acquiescence. British escalation followed the path first of deploying additional forces; then that of declaring an extension of the area of conflict to a radius of 200 miles; next of raising the level both of sophistication and of violence, to which Argentina responded in kind. After the sinking of HMS

SHEFFIELD Britain had a choice: to fight it out at the level and within the area already established, or to extend the conflict, both politically and geographically, by attacking airfields on the mainland of Argentina.

All forms of escalation encounter the same inherent objection. Their repercussions are difficult to limit. Sometimes this can be done. The Cuban Missile crisis of 1962 started at the highest level – what was perceived as a Soviet nuclear threat to the United States – and was actually lowered to an American naval blockade of Cuba. American and Soviet naval escalation during the 1973 Arab–Israeli War never went beyond confrontation. In both cases the two sides had multiple preoccupations. It is more dangerous when one of the contestants is single-minded.

Extending the conflict is a particularly risky form of escalation and seldom successful. The American decision to supplement the defence of South Korea by invading the North brought in China with consequences that were nearly disastrous. This experience probably imposed some restraint in Vietnam, but such extension as was attempted – threats against China, bombing the North, the invasion of Cambodia – was counter-productive. Israel has lost as much as she has gained by attempts to carry the conflict to the territory of her Arab neighbours. In the last thirty-five years it is hard to produce a clear-cut example of a conflict that has been successfully resolved by widening the area of fighting, attacking targets unrelated to the dispute or increasing the number of participants. On the other hand, Confrontation with Indonesia (1963–6) is an instance of ultimate victory and an exceptionally low casualty rate rewarding the resistance of successive British governments to the arguments urged upon them by their military advisers in favour of extending the conflict.

This kind of escalation will nevertheless seem tempting whenever, as often happens, it is open to only one side. In the Falklands crisis, for instance, Britain was physically capable of attacking the mainland of Argentina, even of employing nuclear weapons for this purpose. The British Isles were beyond the reach of Argentine forces. This was a misleading argument in that particular case. Attacks on mainland airfields, the expedient suggested at the time, might have been militarily advantageous (though bombing seldom achieves the predicted result) but the political damage to Britain would almost certainly have exceeded the losses to the Argentine Air Force. Even the military balance might have suffered from the predictable attrition of support from Britain's allies and the new flow of assistance to Argentina. It is

one of the curious paradoxes of contemporary political preconceptions that any success achieved by covert operations against
Argentine airfields would have been much less damaging.

LIMITATION AND DIFFUSION

All the preceding arguments, with their cumulative emphasis on the
extent to which other factors can reduce the value of aggregate
resources as a measure of maritime power, might be challenged as
being relevant only to limited conflicts. Surely, it might be contended,
aggregate resources must be decisive in total war.

There are three answers to this objection: maritime conflicts do tend
to be limited; the rôle of maritime forces in total war is uncertain;
decision is an unreal concept in total war.

For 37 years all maritime conflicts have been limited. Operations
around the Falklands were the first example in that period, the longest
in modern history, of anything that could reasonably be described –
and even that description is not uncontested – as a naval war. It was
certainly limited: partly by the capabilities of the two contestants, but
still more by their deliberate, political choice. Britain did not overtly
attack the mainland of Argentina or Argentine warships in territorial
waters. Argentina did not attempt a wider war against British
merchant shipping or reprisals against British nationals in their power.
Prisoners, with few exceptions, were freely returned. Representatives
of the media enjoyed a surprising liberty to report and comment from
hostile territory. The Red Cross was accorded a rare respect. If any
war can be considered civilised, this was one. The casualties of 74 days
admittedly exceeded those in three years of Confrontation with
Indonesia (1963–6), but they were less than those of one day's fighting
in Vietnam.

The limited character of the only naval war in recent history was
scarcely an accident. Conflict at sea is inherently more controllable
than it is on land or in the air. Civilian populations, for instance, need
not suffer unless a deliberate decision is taken to make them the
targets of attack. Warships can pose, and sustain, an implicit threat
without a single warlike act. They can deploy on the neutral ground of
the high seas and, if need be, conduct their operations without even an
infringement of territorial rights. Their ability to wait allows the
government that controls their movements to gain time: for reflection,
for other preparations, for diplomacy, for negotiations. Above all,

warships are easily withdrawn, even when they have actually been engaged in conflict. Maritime power is such a flexible instrument that it is inevitably the tool of choice, whenever circumstances permit, for the government intending the threat or use of limited force.

On the other hand, its value in total war has declined. The classical advantages celebrated by Mahan disappeared with the invulnerability of the superior fleet. Nobody will ever again be able to write, about any navy, that famous sentence: 'Those far distant, storm-beaten ships, upon which the Grand Army never looked, stood between it and the dominion of the world.'[9] Today the nuclear missile is the trump that can destroy any naval ace – and much else beside. Nor does it make much difference that some of those missiles would be launched from submarines: it is the impact that counts, not the source.

Of course, it is possible to imagine a war that was neither about 'the dominion of the world' nor limited; that did not involve a direct clash of the Super Powers or the use of nuclear weapons; in which no holds were barred by the participants. It is unlikely, for instance, that those concerned in the Arab–Israeli wars of 1967 and 1973 regarded either as limited. The difficulty is to construct a scenario in which such a war is decided by maritime power. The land is no longer as dependent on the sea – for most countries – as it used to be. And the imposition of maritime constraints is now more liable to encounter an effective riposte of terrestrial origin.

The difficulty is even greater if the assumption is general conventional war. It is possible to envisage a war between NATO and the Warsaw Pact in which both sides refrain from the use of nuclear weapons, but the idea that such a war might be confined to the sea or decided by the outcome of naval operations seems unreal. Limitation is a political rather than a military concept. It may involve restricting the objective or the extent or the level of the conflict: it could scarcely mean that two great Alliances would embark on general war, yet allow the outcome to depend on a gladiatorial contest at sea. General war, if it occurs, is bound to include offensives by land and air and these are likely to lead to nuclear escalation or to be terminated by negotiation before the balance of aggregate maritime resources has time to exercise any significant influence on the outcome of the conflict.

In the discussion of nuclear war, admittedly, much attention has been given to the employment of submarines equipped with ballistic missiles and the suggestion has been heard that a 'withholding strategy' might eventually confer a decisive role on the largest surviving submarine force. If this occurred and if the event reflected the initial naval balance, aggregate resources might ultimately emerge as a true measure of maritime power. By that time, however, the result would probably be of little interest to anyone outside New Zealand.

As for deterrence, this is exclusively seaborne only in Britain, whose strategy is entirely dependent on the proposition that, in a narrow range of specific contingencies, her threat to employ appropriate force would dissuade the Kremlin from using the overwhelming force permitted by the far greater aggregate resources of the Soviet Union. But nuclear deterrence is too complex and diffuse a concept for incidental treatment here.

Instead, it may reasonably be conceded that, as maritime conflict loses its limited character, so the importance of aggregate resources tends to increase. Up to a point. That point is the entry into play of the full and mutually opposed resources of the Super Powers. It is conceivable that two lesser powers, or one lesser power and a Super Power could engage in a maritime conflict that would be decided by the balance of aggregate resources. But, once that conflict reaches the stage of *folie à deux*, it is no longer reasonable to suppose that it could remain primarily maritime, that it could continue to be limited or that it could have any meaningfully decisive outcome. Naval forces might play a part in the fighting, but would scarcely have more political significance than Brünnhilde riding her horse into the flames in the last act of *Götterdämmerung*.

CONCLUSION

Much analysis has thus returned us to our starting point. Maritime power can not be reliably measured intrinsically or by static comparisons between the aggregate resources of one nation and those of another, but only in the context of some particular dispute. Aggregate resources are significant only insofar as other constraints allow them to be translated into appropriate force. Naturally this does sometimes happen. Only the United States, for instance, could have stretched a chain of aircraft carriers the length of the Mediterranean to provide seaborne staging-posts for aircraft to reinforce Israel during the 1973 War. Nor could the American purpose have been met without these carriers: the European members of NATO had refused to provide the necessary facilities on land. One could go further. The chances of finding an appropriate use for maritime power tend to increase with aggregate resources, and escalation, unlike other factors, favours the big fleet.

This tendency, however, is subject to numerous exceptions and is, at best, a very broad brush affair. Obviously a Super Power has many more opportunities – in terms of distance, time and the level of conflict – than a minor power. If these advantages are not outweighed by lack of motivation or vulnerability to the international environment, they may prove decisive – in many disputes, but not in all. It is in the middle range that differences in aggregate resources are most misleading.

This is a point on which the Falklands War is peculiarly instructive. If we make a static comparison of aggregate resources on the basis of the *Military Balance*, Britain enjoyed a 3:1 superiority in major surface combat vessels; an immeasurable superiority (thanks to the possession of nuclear submarines) below the surface; an advantage in the air of at least 4:1; a quantitative advantage in ground troops of 1½:1. Britain spent on defence nearly eight times as much as Argentina.[10] And Britain has submarine-launched ballistic nuclear missiles that could have devastated Argentine cities without the remotest possibility of an Argentine response in kind. Any statistician must have concluded, without even considering relative economic resources, that the outcome of any conflict was so foregone as to make its occurrence inconceivable.

The war that actually occurred and the course it took revealed more than bad political judgment in both Buenos Aires and London: it also demonstrated the irrelevance of such comparisons. It was a near-run thing. If the operational radius of the Argentine Air Force had been a little longer, if all their bombs had been correctly fused, if CANBERRA had been sunk, if INVINCIBLE's engine trouble had proved irremediable, if a dozen other very conceivable contingencies had occurred: the outcome would have been rather different. Distance and time were adverse to the British; the level of conflict and the international environment were at best neutral. In the end it was motivation that counted, but in a paradoxical manner. On the merits of the dispute Britain was readier to compromise than Argentina. When it came to the crunch – fight or surrender – only the Argentine Air Force were prepared to match the resolution which the contest evoked from the British, whether at the cloistered heights of Downing Street or among the sailors – many of them civilian – marines, airmen and soldiers who actually had to do the job.

In the last resort motivation was more important than resources.

The Americans failed to rescue their hostages in 1980 partly because they were not willing to risk one of their dozen aircraft carriers at the head of the Persian Gulf. The British succeeded because they were willing to risk all the carriers they had – and a good deal else beside. This is not a moral judgment. A Super Power can accept and digest incidental humiliations unacceptable to a medium power whose efforts to remain in that precarious category depend more on reputation than on measurable assets. It is nevertheless an instructive comparison.

Maritime power is today diffused for two reasons. The first is technological. No single ship, not even the most sophisticated fleet, is today so superior to all potential adversaries as to enjoy immunity at sea. Both are vulnerable, in the right circumstances, to weapons that are cheap, readily available and widely diffused. Maritime superiority can still be achieved, but it is a condition much more expensive, less reliable and more precisely tailored to the circumstances of particular disputes than it used to be.

In terms of pure technology, the gap between a Super Power and a minor nation may seem wider than it has ever been. Militarily, at all but the highest levels of combat, it has probably narrowed. What is even more important is the general levelling-up which has taken place throughout the world in standards of political and administrative organisation. Here international relativities have definitely not been preserved. The ability to handle, or to adapt to, the use of force as a political instrument has become more widely diffused and less uneven. The watershed was probably the AMETHYST incident of 1949, which ended nearly a century's British naval dominance of Chinese rivers. It had been both technically and militarily possible, for much of this period, for a battery of field artillery to deny the Yangtse to British warships. AMETHYST was greatly superior to the traditional gunboats. That was the year in which political organisation and motivation translated hypothesis into fact. Every succeeding year has sharpened the relevance of that earlier question concerning maritime power: power to do what?

The answer tends to favour those purposes which are negative rather than positive and which are restricted in their scope. It is easier to deny some use of the sea than to control, protect or exploit it. Denial is more efficacious if it does not have to be general, but is directed to a particular use, in a limited area and for a short period of time. Maritime power is most economically employed when a single-minded state equipped with some sophisticated weapons seeks to deny to a distant antagonist the temporary use of adjacent waters within easy range of shore-based aircraft and artillery. Turkish defence of the Dardanelles in 1915, relying on nothing more sophisticated than mines and fortress guns, was an early example.

This was a fairly extreme case of everything but the comparison of aggregate resources favouring the coastal state, but it was complicated, as all real examples inevitably are, by human error. The Falklands War, as we have seen, was nearer the break-even point. The Vietnam War was the outstanding instance, in recent times, of the weight of aggregate resources allowing a distant state to achieve protracted maritime dominance in coastal waters. Even that was imperfect – and not only because no degree of success at sea, or from the sea, could have secured American objectives. Political factors prevented more than a momentary interruption of seaborne traffic to Haiphong, and the coastal waters of South Vietnam and Cambodia were never completely denied to the enemy.

Naturally the future could produce a different case: a clear triumph for aggregate resources of the kind achieved, with so much difficulty, delay and sacrifice, in the Pacific campaign of the United States against Japan from 1941 to 1945. In the last 37 years, however, it is hard to identify a significant dispute in which the factors of location, time, motivation, international environment and level of conflict were not, collectively or individually, more important than aggregate resources. Nor is it easy to imagine the future conflict that might invalidate that proposition.

In the last two decades of the twentieth century maritime power is squeezed between two constraints. At the bottom end of the scale other factors restrict the ability of the strongest naval power to employ appropriate force at sea in pursuit of political aims. At the top end force ceases to be recognisably maritime or to have any attainable political objectives.

In between, of course, there remains a large spectrum of conflict in which force can, and will, appropriately be exercised at or from the sea. But there is no single factor which determines whether this force will be appropriate or whether it will prevail in any particular dispute. Maritime power is diffused because the results of its application are inherently uncertain. This is what makes it widely worth having. If God was always on the side of the big fleet, fewer countries would bother to maintain small ones. As it is, many states enjoy maritime power for one purpose, a few for several, none for all. It is potentially useful at many levels, infallible at none.

Twenty years ago Lord Strang enunciated a proposition deeply disturbing to all critics of the excessive pragmatism of British foreign policy. 'The number of ways in which the national interest can be damaged by foreign action is legion. To find the best way to meet each of them will call for an individual exercise, separately conducted.'[11] As a general statement it is incomplete and unacceptable. But it does have an uncomfortable relevance to the existence and exercise of maritime power. The preceding analysis has produced many instances to suggest when and where and how and why and to what extent that power might be both manifest and useful. It has not answered the initial question, only emphasised the importance of asking it, again and again and from scratch, in every individual dispute.

Power to do what?

3 Interdependence: a Drug of Addiction?

Interdependence is the convenient slogan commonly employed today to explain and justify Britain's external policies – economic, military and political – the euphemism that masks the reality of dependence and of the progressive, if still partial, surrender of British sovereignty.

The word can, of course, be given other meanings. One of them is an equilibrium in which, for any given state, the dependence of national decisions on foreign views is balanced by the dependence of foreign decisions on national views. An equilibrium, however, can only be distinguished from qualified independence, on the one hand, or qualified dependence, on the other, if the point of balance can be accurately determined. In the rough relativities of politics a concept so absolute and so imprecise as interdependence is as hard to establish in principle as it is to attain in practice. It is at best an aspiration (as in de Gaulle's proposal for an American–British–French directorate of the Alliance) and more often an excuse.[1]

Interdependence can also be regarded as describing one of the characteristics of international society. As Macaulay put it in 1842:

> In order that he [Frederick the Great] might rob a neighbour whom he had promised to defend, black men fought on the coast of Coromandel, and red men scalped each other by the Great Lakes of North America.[2]

The significance of this interdependence, however, does not derive from its objective nature, but from the differing responses of particular states. We are all individually dependent on electricity, but for some of us this is a luxury that operates the television set; for others it is so vital that we instal an emergency generator – if we can afford it; while some aged pensioners can neither pay the quarterly account nor change a bulb without assistance.

Dependence and independence are more useful concepts. Neither is

55

ever absolute, but they provide the two ends of a scale which offers one way of comparing the nations of the world. Near the middle, of course, the gradations are often too small to be read with much precision or objectivity, but nobody would deny that the Soviet Union is more independent than Gibraltar. The test is perceived vulnerability to the external environment and the methods chosen for reducing that vulnerability. Neither is objectively determined. It could be argued, for instance, that the Soviet leaders perceive their country as more vulnerable than it really is. Their preference for self-reliance as the appropriate response is, however, matched by Switzerland, for whom even membership of the United Nations seems an unacceptable derogation from independence.

Naturally objective factors do influence any choice between the advantages and constraints of external assistance or the freedom and cost of self-reliance. The conventional wisdom, for instance, regards the dependence so characteristic of Britain's post-war policies as an inevitable response to objectively established changes in the international environment. An alternative view, which this article seeks to explore, is that dependence, dignified with the name of interdependence, was an option which Britain, together with some other countries, happened to prefer. There were strong arguments to support the choice, but they were neither universally accepted nor carried to such extreme conclusions.

France, for instance, does not rely on anyone else for her nuclear weapons; allow foreign military bases on her territory; commit her forces to foreign command; run to the International Monetary Fund for loans with strings; often conform to decisions reached without her consent; or send her prime ministers and opposition leaders to kiss hands in Washington on the occasion of their appointment.

France, admittedly, is now a richer country than Britain. Is this cause or effect? The attraction of external assistance is that it reduces the need for domestic effort, a therapeutic effect which may be indispensable if the effort in question is manifestly impossible, but which can become habit-forming when it is not.

Britain's need for external assistance has naturally varied from one period, and one contingency, to another, but has tended to increase as fast as Britain's strength in relation to other countries has diminished. The root cause seems to have been relative economic decline. That process began over a century ago. Some of the reasons were external and obvious: the maturing industrialisation of countries with larger populations and greater natural resources. The internal reasons, generally agreed to have been no less important, are more controversial. Scientific principles suggest that preference should be accorded to those explanations first advanced as predictions rather than to retrospective analysis.

In 1870, for instance, Lyon Playfair warned the Philosophical Institution of Edinburgh that 'this country is losing her position among manufacturing nations – the industrial supremacy of England is endangered for lack of knowledge, in spite of the practical aptitudes of her people'.[3] He had profited by the growing importance of his public position to disseminate similar warnings ever since 1852 and he continued to do so until his death in 1898. His words were not unheeded, but they evoked insufficient response from their complacent audience. In 1871, after all, the British output of pig iron exceeded that of the rest of the world.[4] Even then, however, steel was becoming more important and the following ratios illustrate Britain's relative decline: US, Germany, Britain (1880) 1:1:1; (1900) 10:6:5; (1913) 4:2:1.[5] What was even more important was that the high technology industries (into which Britain might have diversified) were being increasingly developed abroad: chemicals, automotive propulsion, electricity, scientific instruments, new inventions. Playfair had all too much reason for his question (to the British Association for the Advancement of Science in 1885):

how is it that we find whole branches of manufacture, when they depend on scientific knowledge, passing away from this country in which they originated, in order to engraft themselves abroad, although their decaying roots remain at home?[6]

In 1983 his question can still be asked and still awaits an answer, though Playfair had indicated his own in 1870:

let me ask you seriously whether you think that this country can continue in a career of prosperity, when she is the only leading state in Europe that is neglecting the higher education of the working classes, and of those men above them whose duty it is to superintend their labour?[7]

Playfair's prescription may have been incomplete – historians have retrospectively suggested additional remedies – but the accuracy of his prognosis has received a confirmation too melancholy to bear recapitulation.[8] Nor did he confine his view that 'the competition of the

world has become a competition of intellect'[9] to the purely economic
sphere. Although personally hostile to the very idea of war and even to
defence expenditure, he attributed the outcome of the Franco-
Prussian War to the fact that illiteracy in France was 28 per cent, but
in Germany only 3 per cent. 'Knowledge is as important as valour in
modern combats.'[10]

It would be going too far to argue that, from the final quarter of the
last century, Britain had a real choice between a domestic process of
drastic modernisation and an external process of alleviating her
difficulties through the acceptance of increasing dependence. Choices
do not exist in practical politics unless those who have to make them
clearly perceive the necessity, the nature, the extent and the feasibility
of the choice. There was such a perception at much the same period in
Japan. So there was, after 1917, in Russia. In both countries,
however, only exceptional circumstances permitted so decisive a
preference for social transformation. It would thus be unfair to judge
British governments by such examples, not least because of the
exorbitant cost in human suffering of Soviet independence. Moreover,
for most of the twentieth century (the two world wars excepted) it was
usually possible for British governments to take the comfortable view
that Britain's problems were sectoral, transitional and of external
origin and that they themselves were already doing as much as could
reasonably be expected to solve them.

Between the Boer War and the Great War, for instance, the Army
and Navy were extensively modernised, education was improved and
certain social reforms initiated. Nothing was done about the economy
(by 1902 Britain was importing steel), but this was not then accepted
as a governmental responsibility and reforms in other fields encountered so much opposition as to suggest that more was politically
impracticable. Only during the two world wars did widespread support exist for drastic change and even this was narrowly focussed on
the immediate objective of military victory. Nor did Playfair's successors, any more than Playfair himself, usually advocate comprehensive
reforms. They wanted changes unacceptable to the conventional wisdom, but they too tended to adopt a sectoral approach. Keynes, for
instance, invited as chairman of an official committee in 1930, 'to
review the present economic condition of Great Britain', came up with
the short-term expedient of 'a revenue tariff – because it will give us a
margin of resources and a breathing-space, under cover of which we
can do other things'.[11] The revenue tariff was eventually adopted and
proved beneficial, but the 'other things' (Keynes had written as early

as 1919 of Britain's need for 'a new industrial birth')[12] were naturally not done.

Imposing a tariff or seeking a foreign loan may alleviate only the symptoms of disease, but do offer a 'quick fix'. Radical reform is usually open to the objection that its results will be slow to appear. Moreover, it often seems easier to persuade other governments to acquiesce in an executive decision or even to take one of their own, than it is to mobilise an entire people for new and socially disturbing exertions. Britain's increasing resort to external assistance for the solution of problems that, to the retrospective gaze, now appear as the progressive symptoms of domestic national decline, may have been regrettable, but it was always understandable.

The first step had the innocent, almost therapeutic character so familiar in the case-histories of addiction: the Anglo-Japanese Alliance of 1902. There was a strong case for it: the 4 British battleships and 16 cruisers on the China Station were not enough to maintain British interests in the Far East against a potential Franco-Russian combination in those waters of 9 battleships and 20 cruisers. The Japanese Alliance did not merely obviate the need for British reinforcements or for new docks at Hong Kong: it eventually permitted the withdrawal of those battleships to strengthen the fleet in home waters. Even the Kaiser, that harsh critic of British policy, conceded that 'at last the noodles have had a lucid interval'.[13] Naturally there was a price to pay, as various admirals and other awkward characters argued at the time: the British position in the Far East was henceforth dependent on Japanese goodwill and (after the victory of Tsushima in 1905) without any corresponding Japanese dependence on British goodwill. Britain's first experience of the drug had nevertheless been reassuring. The second Anglo-Japanese Alliance was concluded in 1905 and the Third in 1911. The side-effects took another decade to reach a level then judged to be unacceptable.

It was under the influence of the initial euphoria that the various arrangements were made that led to British continental commitment in European war. This was a major departure from the British tradition of financing other people to do the fighting. Whether or not the process was avoidable, a point which will continue to be debated until the arrival of the Third World War, the outcome was profoundly damaging and revived a form of dependence unknown to Britain since the seventeenth century: on foreign, in this case American, economic assistance.

In the aftermath of the First World War Britain was confronted with a curious dilemma: her two naval rivals were the United States and Japan. Alliance with the first as insurance against war with the second was unattainable and the opposite combination seemed undesirable. Yet Britain could not match the formidable building pro-gramme threatened by the United States against – it was scarcely con-cealed – Britain herself. The Great War had proved as profitable to the United States as had the Napoleonic Wars to Britain and the economic ratio between the two countries was 3:1 in American favour. The Washington Naval Treaty of 1922 rescued Britain from an arms-race, but at the price of conceding naval dominance in the Far East to a Japan whose goodwill had to be sacrificed with the alliance that had proved so useful in the First World War. That was the worst kind of dependence, for British exposure to Japan was not compensated by even a promise of American support. But the alternative proposed in 1920 by Jellicoe (who regarded war with Japan as inevitable) was more than a declining British economy could support: a Far Eastern Fleet of 8 battleships, 8 battle-cruisers and 4 carriers. And nobody seems to have suggested abandoning such commitments as could no longer be defended.

Britain's economy continued to languish. The rejection in 1930 of the proposals put forward by Mosley (then a Labour Minister) for its regeneration through planned foreign trade, public direction of industry and credit-financed expansion was, as A. J. P. Taylor says, 'a decisive, though negative, event in British history'.[14] The natural sequel in 1931 was Britain's first peace-time acceptance of economic and political dependence. On 23 August Messrs J. P. Morgan & Co. of New York informed the British Government that American bankers would consent to rescue the pound provided that the political terms already tentatively accepted by a reluctant Cabinet also 'had the sincere approval and support of the Bank of England and the City generally'.[15] The future still had similar humiliations in store for Britain, but this was the last occasion on which shame actually brought down a British government.

So far open dependence (for anyone reluctant to adopt a statistical approach to hypothetical questions) had been confined to periods of crisis. The turning point was the Second World War, not just because of the sheer extent and range of Britain's dependence on the United States, but because, for the first time, the British people were taught to regard such dependence as natural, lasting and even virtuous. Admittedly the Churchillian rhetoric was primarily intended for the Americans, but the idea was disseminated in Britain as widely as jeeps in the British army. 'Give us the tools, and we will finish the job'.[16] was a fine phrase for public consumption, but Churchill knew as well as anyone else that a great deal more than Lend-Lease would be required before Britain, the Soviet Union and the United States could defeat a self-reliant Germany. She had, after all, drastically transformed her own economy and society for the specific purpose of war during those 'locust years' which Britain frittered away in self-deluding reliance on imperial preference, the League of Nations, collective security and the French army. It is unfortunate that those nations who pull themselves up by their own boot-straps so often do so from reprehensible motives, but need the Devil have all the best tunes?

By 1945 the British had come to take Lend-Lease so much for granted that they were genuinely shocked at its termination, resented the 'strings' attached to the subsequent American Loan and accepted Marshall Aid as no more than their due. Britain became, and has remained, a client of the United States.

What is a client state? In Britain's case it means, first, dependence on the United States for the management of the British economy. The extent of that dependence was most brutally illustrated in 1956, when the withdrawal of American goodwill resulted in a run on sterling, the refusal of assistance by the American-dominated International Monetary Fund (IMF) and the abandonment of Britain's Suez adventure (in which France had been willing to persist). The circumstances were then admittedly exceptional, but the loans and credit facilities (together with their political conditions) actually obtained by Britain in 1957, 1961, 1967 and 1976 from the IMF were no less dependent on American goodwill. So was management of the British financial crises of 1964 and 1966 or the devaluation of 1967. In many of these instances much emphasis was given at the time to multilateral cooperation in rescuing Britain from her temporary financial difficulties. Efforts were made to represent these transactions as no more than the give and take inseparable from an universal and inevitable 'interdependence' in international financial relations. From time to time examples were produced of British cooperation in smoothing out the transitional exchange problems of other countries. It never happened, however, that Britain had a decisive voice in the grant of financial assistance to another important country; that she was able to impose political conditions (not even to prohibit the purchase of arms with British money by Argentina in 1983); that the United States – or France, Germany, Japan or a dozen other countries – were dependent on British goodwill. It was always a one-sided relationship.

Part of the price was British deference towards American policies in general. South-East Asia provides an interesting example. From 1954 onwards successive British governments doubted, on different grounds and with varying degrees of conviction, the wisdom of the American adventure in Indo-China. Only Eden risked open, if limited, opposition at the Geneva Conference of 1954 and he paid for his temerity at Suez in 1956. The lesson was learnt and later British reservations, even when fuelled by the strong feelings of the Labour Party between 1964 and 1970, never found more overt expression than the pinpricks, not even intended as such, of the futile Wilson 'initiatives'.

Meanwhile Britain was involved in a South-East Asian conflict of her own – Confrontation with Indonesia from 1963 to 1966. This eventually proved to be the most successful limited war anyone had fought since 1945 – a three-year total of casualties less than that of one day's fighting in Vietnam or the whole of the much briefer Falklands War. It also produced a peace settlement that has so far lasted seventeen years. At the time, however, the American preference for appeasing Sukarno (then regarded in Washington as a potential anti-Communist leader) was vigorously pressed on the British Government at every level. Even the author used to be telephoned at home before breakfast by the United States Embassy. That was what interdependence meant in the sixties.

Of course, Britain's dependence on the United States was qualified. Whereas Australia had to send troops to Vietnam and France could voice open disapproval of American policy, Britain occupied a middle position. In Vietnam she got away with expressions of sympathy and gestures of non-military support. Malaysia was encouraged to respond to American initiatives and to take part in futile negotiations, but British troops continued their defence of Borneo. Such compromises are only sensible in peripheral issues. It is when American policies impinge on vital British interests that the exertion of British influence in Washington needs to be uninhibited. Unfortunately this is a condition subject to more than economic constraints.

Since 1939 it has been not merely the management of Britain's economy, but her defence against external military challenge, that has depended on American goodwill. This military dependence has, to a considerable degree, been imposed by circumstances beyond Britain's control: the emergence of the Soviet Union as an unfriendly Super Power with resources that no British effort could have matched.

Britain's only alternative to dependence on allies was the neutrality preferred by Sweden or Switzerland. This was not an option acceptable to British public opinion in the post-war era, nor were other allies of any value then available. Reliance on the United States was, therefore, initially almost inevitable. It has nevertheless proved so habit-forming that this dependence is now more extensive than was originally foreseen. The constraints it has imposed on Britain's policy and strategy, no less than on the structure, deployment and equipment of Britain's own forces, have actually reduced Britain's chances of responding effectively to certain kinds of threat below the level of total war.

For instance, British nuclear weapons offer a chance of excluding the British Isles from the nuclear battlefield in a territorially limited nuclear war, because the Soviet Union might hesitate to risk the loss of Moscow by bombarding Britain, if they expected the United States to respect the immunity of Soviet territory as long as the continental United States remained similarly inviolate. This chance, however, can only be diminished by the presence of American nuclear weapons, particularly those intended for limited war, in the British Isles. Deterrence demands an ability to reward abstention that is no less assured than the capacity to punish aggression. Without a British monopoly of nuclear weapons in the British Isles the British Government can scarcely count on being considered in Moscow as *un interlocuteur valable.*

Unfortunately British dependence on the United States for ballistic missiles and other essential components of the British nuclear deterrent makes it difficult for Britain to exclude American nuclear weapons under American control or to close any of the 64 American military bases that make the British Isles such an obvious target for those Soviet missiles which can not, in any case, cross the Atlantic.

France, having herself developed a truly independent deterrent, has no such inhibitions and can cheerfully support the deployment of American missiles anywhere outside France. Her chances of escaping the direct impact of territorially limited nuclear war are undiminished – and greater than Britain's.

This too was predicted.

Late in 1947, when it was suggested that Britain might rely on the United States for the maintenance of her nuclear striking force, Lord Tedder, Chief of the Air Staff, voiced a general feeling when he replied that this would involve a close military alliance with the

United States in which Britain would be merely a temporary advance base, would involve complete subservience to United States policy and would render Britain completely impotent in negotiations with Russia or any other nation.[17]

Military dependence is most obvious in nuclear strategy, because the decision to launch American missiles or aircraft, wherever they are stationed, will inevitably be taken in Washington. No government, when faced by the mortal choice of nuclear war, can be expected to subordinate national interest to foreign wishes, whatever undertakings may previously have been given.[18] In 1973, for instance, in the course of a dispute with the Soviet Union not involving the rest of NATO but concerning the Arab–Israeli War, United States forces throughout the world were placed on the alert (DEFCON III except for the Sixth Fleet, which went to DEFCON II, the highest grade short of war). According to American sources the three US Air Force strike bases and the POLARIS submarine facility in Britain were placed on the alert before responsible British authorities were even informed, let alone consulted.[19] As long as there are American nuclear weapons in the British Isles, British survival will continue to depend on decisions taken in Washington, perhaps in the course of quarrels to which Britain is not a party.

Britain's other commitments to NATO are usually represented as no more than her share of an interdependence common to all the Allies. In fact, of course, some members of NATO are more equal than others. As Alliance strategy is ultimately dependent on an American threat to employ nuclear weapons, the United States have a power of veto, as well as a capacity for initiation, which is not generally shared. France is best placed to abstain from any conflict which, in her judgment, does not directly threaten French interests. Britain's dependence is perhaps the greatest of all, for she not only has foreign bases on her soil, but the bulk of her army and much of her air force in Germany. There may never be a crisis in which Britain wants to disengage from NATO, nor would this necessarily be in her interests, but she would undoubtedly find the process more difficult than would some of her Allies.

It can, of course, be argued that any threat to any member of NATO must be a general threat, as dangerous to Britain as to anyone else; that such threats can only be deterred or resisted by an united Alliance; and that unity depends on locking all the members into a permanent framework of deployment and command as well as treaty obligation. In the somewhat masochistic language of the Ministry of Defence 'it is politically important that all allies should share the risks and burdens of providing for deterrence and defence'.[20] The assumption may be correct, but it is worth nothing that nobody else is so deeply committed to the practical application of the British conclusion. Even the Germans deploy their forces only to defend their own soil.

To the conventional wisdom the defence of Britain is 'subsumed' – always a suspect verb – by the collective strategy of NATO. 'The direct defence of the United Kingdom base', for instance, 'is obviously vital' as 'a forward base for operations in the Atlantic, a main base for operations in the Channel and North Sea and a rear base for operations on the Continent.'[21] This curious conception of one's own country would be hard to match elsewhere in the world. Perhaps in East Germany?

The Falklands War may seem an exception to the general principle of British military dependence, but did not invalidate this concept. It would never have happened if the defence of British interests had not been subordinated to the requirements of NATO. Secondly, it could only be fought because the reduction of the Royal Navy to the 'small ASW force destined to protect the first European resupply convoy',[22] which was how Sir John Nott seems to have interpreted the requirements of the American Supreme Commander, had not then been completed. Thirdly, the process had gone far enough to make the war a 'near-run thing' in which Britain might not have succeeded without the rather bare minimum of American goodwill which the operation actually enjoyed. Military action in support of British national interests – even for the maintenance of internal security in Northern Ireland – usually requires the diversion of forces committed to NATO and trained and equipped for the needs of the Alliance.

The conflicting requirements of national and collective purposes usually become obvious only in time of crisis. Then the forces of political dissent may be stimulated by the conditions of an IMF loan or by plans for the installation of new American missiles. What is more important is the intellectual conditioning which forty years of dependence have imposed on successive generations of British politicians, military leaders, officials and the entire Establishment, many academics included. During the Spanish Civil War, when Britain was still a Great Power, one Spanish Captain related how often his confrontations with the Royal Navy brought tears of rage to his eyes and how he nevertheless had to tell his officers: 'We must be prudent, we can not worsen our relations with England'.[23] He has had his revenge. Whitehall and Westminister have long been dominated, to an extent that has to be experienced to be appreciated, by the primacy of good relations with the United States.

This 'special', 'natural', 'close' (there are fashions in adjectives) relationship is unequal. The United States are not dependent on Britain. Naturally it is convenient to have bases and facilities without tiresome strings. A second fiddle can often usefully enhance the harmony of the American theme. There are advantages to the United States worth their cost, as there are for the Soviet Union in keeping Cuba afloat. Prudential considerations are reinforced by custom, tradition, the ties of a common language and cultural history. The influence of association, on a footing of notional equality, during the Second World War is not quite dead. Britain may now seem less important in Washington than Germany or Japan or even that awkward customer, France, but she still gets more consideration than, strictly speaking, she deserves. So, in Moscow, does Finland, who shows greater deference than Britain, but makes fewer material concessions.

British dependence is real, but is it also desirable or even inevitable?

There can be no undisputed answer to these questions. In 1945 opponents of the American Loan denounced its acceptance as 'an economic Munich', to which Keynes retorted that the alternative was 'starvation corner'. Today's advocates of greater economic independence are accused of proposing a 'siege economy'. At any given moment there is a choice, even if this is not always perceived as such, between the immediate benefits of foreign goodwill and its ultimate cost. Moreover, this choice is always complicated by political and sentimental considerations of a different kind from what some regard as the strictly economic or military arguments.

For instance, many of today's British supporters of 'Autarkie' are much influenced by their anxiety to introduce or, in some cases, to resist certain social changes in Britain. It is partly because they expect their internal measures to lead to the loss of foreign confidence and goodwill that they want, so far as possible, to free the British economy from foreign constraints and to insulate it against international repercussions. Their opponents, on the other hand, are not only more impressed by the strength of these constraints and by British vulnerability to repercussions: they also regard the existence of constraints and the danger of repercussions as buttressing the kind of social structure and domestic political orientation they prefer for Britain.

The old-fashioned patriots who resent British dependence on foreigners are balanced by those representatives of a more recent conventional wisdom, who deprecate nationalism and see dependence as leading to the ideal of interdependence and the greatest good of the greatest number. Neither those who consider dependence undesirable nor those who accept it as inevitable are always actuated solely, or even mainly, by anxiety to strengthen Britain's international position.

Confusion is worse compounded because the interaction of economic and military arguments cuts across the natural division between nationalists and internationalists. Some of the former would be glad to see Britain out of the European Economic Community and paddling her own commercial canoe, if they did not fear that this would lead to withdrawal from NATO, to neutralism and eventually to People's Democracy. Some of the latter regard the nuclear strategy of NATO as exposing Britain to needless danger and to involvement in conflicts unrelated to her own survival, yet see Community membership as so vital for Britain's future that concessions may have to be made to the strategic views of its more important members. There is, at present, no important political support for the idea that Britain should be able both to operate her own economy and society as she wishes and also to attempt her own defence, let alone for the drastic internal changes such objectives might require. Perhaps – the point will be further considered – this is an impossible ideal, but the absence of a comprehensive strategy is worth noting – and not only by advocates of independence. Even a genuinely internationalist course would require an integrated approach to economic, military, political and social problems not now reflected in the spectrum of British party conflict.

Compromise is as traditionally British as its results are historically unsatisfactory, but compromise there is obviously going to be. How might it be slanted?

It would clearly be unrealistic, in view of the present fragmentation of British political attitudes, to expect much support for arguments that dependence was intrinsically either desirable or undesirable. Dependence can only be judged by its contribution, whether positive or negative, to some objective generally accepted as possessing overriding importance. The obvious candidate is the survival of the British people.

Survival is not exposed to any direct economic threat in the timescale of politicians and their voters. Even if 'it is inevitable that the decline of British economic power will continue unabated',[24] it will long be possible to argue that decline as a nation compared to other nations, even absolute decline over five or ten years, masks actual improvement in the living standards of the British people compared to those of their parents and grandparents. The efforts of economists to sound a tocsin have fallen on deaf ears and are unlikely to command a popular audience in the foreseeable future.

The threat of war is quite another matter. This already arouses sufficient apprehension to constitute a significant factor in British politics. It is a threat which could become immediate at very short notice. If it did, as Magnus Clarke argues convincingly in *The Nuclear Destruction of Britain*, the survival of the British people would be at risk and, in some circumstances, improbable.[25] There is thus a strong case for holding that dependence is desirable for Britain if it reduces the threat of war, undesirable if it increases that threat.

In principle, of course, it can do either; in practice, the problem is to select the most advantageous position on the sliding scale between the dependence that helps to deter some threats and the independence that helps to escape exposure to others. This demands a difficult and uncertain judgment of the likely nature of the threat. It can be argued, for instance, that any war threatening the survival of the British people would necessarily be total and general. If that assumption is correct, it does not matter that dependence on the United States has made the British Isles a more obvious target for attack and largely transferred to Washington what might otherwise have been a British choice between accepting national destruction and making concessions. Nobody in the northern hemisphere would escape the consequences of total and general war, so Britain's only hope is that the retaliatory power of the United States will deter the Soviet Union from initiating holocaust. Similar conclusions could be drawn from the assumption that Britain is so natural a focus of Soviet hostility that only the fear of American retaliation has prevented the Soviet Union from exercising her undoubted capacity to destroy the British Isles.

These are somewhat improbable assumptions. So is the opposite view that Britain would be immune from all risk of destruction or coercion if she adopted the neutrality preferred by Austria, Finland, Sweden or Switzerland. The British people lack the disciplined self-effacement needed for genuine neutrality, and Britain, even in decline, is still too important a country for her alignment to escape the interest and competing pressures of both Super Powers and the resentment, even the active resentment, of one or other of them.

Between these extremes a third view is more plausible. The history of the last 37 years suggests that limited war and coercive diplomacy are more likely threats than total and general war. Britain is perhaps over-committed to deterrence of the gravest but least likely threat, under-insured against lesser but more probable contingencies. Dependence is not a serious handicap for the former, but it is for the latter and for reasons that are two sides of the same coin: dependence could suck Britain into limited American quarrels that would not otherwise concern her, yet restrict British freedom of manoeuvre in those quarrels which did not engage the full power of the United States.

Switzerland, for instance, has preserved as much freedom as anyone can to avoid involvement in the quarrels of others, but has taken active steps to reduce their repercussions on herself. Swiss precautions against nuclear fall-out are greatly superior to British.

For Britain, however, a better example is France, who has paid a smaller premium for the deterrence of total war and preserved her right of choice in limited war. The appropriate British compromise would be: no foreign bases in the British Isles; a limited but independent nuclear deterrent; an improved capacity for the conventional defence of the British Isles and Narrow Seas; a contingent, predominantly maritime and not irrevocable commitment to NATO. In the game of international poker Britain needs to be able to raise the ante to significant levels, but can expect no profit from a permanent commitment to the maximum stake.

Could this be done? It was certainly once possible, as Britain demonstrated by her reaction to the McMahon Act of 1946, by which the United States repudiated their war-time agreements and prohibited the exchange of atomic information with Britain. Not only did Britain then proceed to the independent development of nuclear weapons, but she became the first country in the world to use nuclear power to generate electricity for public consumption. Indeed, the post-war decade in Britain was remarkable for its initiative and innovation. Seeds of many kinds were sown for a national renaissance which never came to full fruition.

Perhaps this was because dependence on the United States continued unabated in other fields. It is tempting to regard the Suez fiasco of 1956 as the turning point in Britain's destiny, for Britain and France were to draw opposite conclusions from that humiliating experience: Britain that she could no longer afford the assertion of independence; France that she must create the basis for it. In 1958, for instance, the French Prime Minister, the travails of the Fourth

Republic notwithstanding, signed the order for the independent production of a French atomic bomb, while de Gaulle's latest biographer
describes the humiliation of Suez as helping to create the conditions
for the General's later return to power.[26] The British Prime Minister,
on the other hand, agreed in 1957 to the installation in East Anglia of
American THOR missiles and, in 1958, the repeal of the McMahon
Act enabled Britain to resume nuclear dependence on the United
States.

In the light of subsequent French achievements, at home and
abroad, economic as well as military, it is difficult to argue that it was
economically impossible for Britain to pursue a more independent
policy after Suez. In 1957, after all, Britain's gross national product
was 50 per cent greater than that of France. Dependence was a British
choice, a political preference.

It would be foolish to suggest only one cause for so complex a
phenomenon, but it is reasonable to put much of the blame on the
addiction to dependence acquired by Britain's rulers – and by all that
numerous class of young administrators, civil and military, who
would later become rulers or advisers to rulers – during the Second
World War. The ability to retain American goodwill was then and
thereafter often a condition for promotion. French experience was
different, thanks to General de Gaulle, who always asserted French
independence in the face of greater obstacles and without regard to the
fury of his more powerful and indispensable allies. His example was
not forgotten even amid the divisions and dependence of the Fourth
Republic and it was entrenched for his successors by what he achieved
for France after his return to power. 'President Mitterand's Socialist
government is adhering to the main lines of de Gaulle's foreign and
defence policies. The basis of them is national independence.'[27]

Can the British leopard now change its dependent spots? So far the
only serious attempt has been to replace dependence on the United
States by dependence on Europe. People forget – indeed many of
them now wish to – how far-reaching were some of the ideas
considered in British political and official circles a dozen years ago:
European political union, European defence cooperation, a common
foreign policy, Anglo-French nuclear collaboration. Behind them all
lay the hope that Britain could recover, as a leading member of an
united Europe, some of the relative power, prosperity and influence
she had lost as an American client. Little progress was made in these
directions even under the initially optimistic Heath administration.
The high water mark (not a spring tide) was perhaps the lead taken by

Britain in stimulating resistance to the hegemony sought by Kissinger in his notorious Year of Europe in 1973. Enthusiasts in Britain hoped for more than Europeans were ready for, but the American-orientated British bureaucracy imposed a constant check on even such progress as might have been possible. Their resistance was greatly strengthened in 1974 by the return of a Labour Government suspicious of Europe and preferring reliance on the United States. All that remained was the hope that membership of the European Community would somehow revive the British economy as – so it was suggested – it had revived those of Britain's European competitors.

Whether European success was due to association or to national effort is a question too complex and controversial for discussion here. The former theory, however, was assumed to be correct, applicable to Britain and made the subject of a prediction duly falsified by experience. In 1971 the British Government of the day declared: 'membership of the enlarged Community will lead to much improved efficiency and productivity in British industry, with a higher rate of investment and a faster growth of real wages'.[28]

Table 1 shows roughly what happened.[29]

TABLE 1

	1960	1970	% Increase 1960–70	1980	% Increase 1970–80
Output per person employed (1975 = 100)	74	94.2	27	108.7	15
Gross domestic fixed capital formation (£million 1975 prices)	11905	19460	62	20761	6
Real personal disposable income (£million 1975 prices)	11488	15313	33	20891	36

It may well be argued that this comparison, quite apart from any statistical fallacies it may embody, is not a fair test because it takes no account of the world depression that developed between 1970 and 1980. On this point the verdict of foreign experts is instructive.

There were three seismic shocks to the world economy: the breakdown of the Bretton Woods monetary system from 1971 to 1973; the explosive rise of world prices of raw materials from 1972 to 1974; and the oil crisis in 1973–74. Very likely the deterioration in Britain's economic performance is related to these external shocks. As already noted, all industrial countries were adversely affected, but the United Kingdom more so than the others. Why? It was not just the occurrence of shocks but British reaction to them that seemed to matter.[30]

This brings us back to our starting-point: the significance of inter-dependence does not derive from its objective nature, but from the differing responses of particular states. British responses to the challenges, whether economic or military, of the external environment have been more dependent than those of other states. They have also been less successful. Britain has, for twenty years, fared worse, by every economic test, than France, West Germany and Japan, the last being the outstanding example of the independent pursuit of economic success by a country needing to import most of its energy and raw materials. Those smaller European countries which avoided economic dependence – Austria, Finland, Norway, Sweden, Switzerland – have long enjoyed higher per capita incomes. Germany and Japan, admittedly, have for years been militarily dependent, but Germany, at least, may claim to gain more than she gives. Montgomery's boast, in 1948, 'at last we had achieved that for which I had been fighting – a decision that in the event of war the British Army would fight on the Continent of Europe'[31] may, thirty-five years later, strike some of his countrymen as a more doubtful benefit.

The economic and military history of nations in any way comparable to Britain exhibits considerable and idiosyncratic differences, but there is little evidence to support any general rule that the acceptance of interdependence, even in the most euphemistic sense of the term, is more rewarding than national exertion animated by national purpose.

This proposition, so cautiously advanced for other nations, may be more confidently asserted of the British. It is not merely that their fortunes have declined in step with their acceptance of dependence: this could be considered a chicken and egg argument. British exertions have also been proportional to the national character of their endeavour. Their finest hour was in the summer of 1940 and the British have never since been so united or so ardent. Even the Falklands episode of 1982 – though war is repugnant and that war was peculiarly unnecessary – brought a pale reflection of the same spirit. The British like to do their own thing.

They have been offered few opportunities in recent years. NATO and the EEC are little less alien and uninspiring to the British than the IMF or GATT. If there is to be a British recovery in international terms, this will have to start at home and be fuelled by a sense of national purpose animated by a leadership perceived as specifically British.

It is not obvious who could provide that leadership. More than one British politician would dearly like to stage a return from Colombey les deux Eglises, but freedom from foreign allegiances and the support of an organised party do not seem to go together. Nobody could achieve full success without a comprehensive programme for drastic domestic change and a Gaullist readiness to run risks abroad. Any realistic prediction[32] must be that the British will continue to accept the supplementary benefits, and accompanying servitudes, of inter-·dependence rather than launch themselves into the adventure of inde-pendence.

It is, of course, possible to envisage a more modest reduction in dependence through the adoption of a deliberately national approach to the conduct of Britain's external relations. The multiplier effect this can have is well illustrated by the example of France. It was the style imposed by General de Gaulle in 1940 which made that country what she is today. The deference which dependence has bred in British governments has increased their dependence. Quarter of a century ago, for instance, Mr Macmillan (now Lord) ensured that American missiles in East Anglia were equipped with the dual-key system for which Mrs Thatcher is now reluctant even to ask.

Nevertheless, before Ministers are seduced by the idea of exploiting Britain's nuisance value and relying on the doctrine of *'l'intendance suivra'*, they should reflect on another essential ingredient of French success. This was consistency of purpose and uniformity of approach. Intransigence over milk makes little impact when combined with acquiescence on missiles. Style is more important than is understood in Britain, but it must reflect rather than replace policy. It must also at least be followed by concrete measures.

Apprehension about the prospects of national survival and disil-lusionment with external economic palliatives may conceivably provide a political base for a new leadership to impart a different slant to compromise. The chances of success are slender, for the time has clearly not yet come for heroic remedies, but both leaders and led will deceive themselves if they imagine that Britain's addiction to depen-dence can even be controlled, let alone reduced, without experiencing some of the unpleasant side-effects of withdrawal.

4 Will Gibraltar be Next?

On Friday, 13 August 1982 a public opinion poll suggested that only 29 per cent of the Spanish people favoured the military seizure of Gibralter.[1] Perhaps the ominous resemblance between the Spanish claim to Gibraltar and the Argentine claim to the Falklands is not destined to be completed by an equally violent climax. Perhaps.

Both territories were disputed by Britain and Spain in eighteenth-century wars and both were eventually ceded to Britain: in the case of Gibraltar by seven separate treaties. Undisturbed British possession began later: 1834 in the Falklands, 1813 in Gibraltar. Undisturbed did not mean undisputed. In 1855 a distinguished Governor of Gibraltar, Sir Robert Gardiner, was forthright in his warning to London:

> It must not be supposed that the Spaniards ever lose hope of repossessing Gibraltar, either by conquest or by stratagem in war, or by negotiation in peace. It would be against nature if they could do so.[2]

That was at the height of Britain's long period of naval ascendancy and unchallenged status as a Great Power. While that endured neither Argentina nor Spain took active steps to press their claims and the only serious military threat to either territory came from Germany: to the Falklands in 1914, to Gibraltar in 1940.

The end of the Second World War introduced a new era: progressive liquidation of the British Empire; decline of the Royal Navy; a campaign against colonialism in the United Nations. Argentina and Spain abandoned legal arguments in favour of the new slogans now in fashion. Both rejected British proposals to submit the dispute to the International Court of Justice, as they did British concern for the wishes of the inhabitants: 'The territory of the Falkland Islands is much more important than the population; the consent or otherwise of the Gibraltarians – is legally and politically irrelevant.'[3]

Both disputes then followed similar courses: mounting pressure by the claimant; increasing British readiness to discuss everything but the

74

essential issue of sovereignty; progressive reduction of deployed British forces.

Spain's geographical proximity, however, enabled her to apply increasing economic coercion to Gibraltar from 1954 onwards. Frontier restrictions deprived the city of some of its labour force, much of its trade and most of its prospects as a tourist centre. Culminating in 1969 in complete border closure, these measures made it unnecessary for Spain to imitate Argentine resort to recurrent naval pinpricks in order to emphasise the seriousness of her claim. The iron fist was nevertheless occasionally visible. Spanish restrictions on flying in the vicinity of Gibraltar (introduced in 1966 and intensified in 1967) created the risk of a confrontation, even an actual clash, involving military aircraft. In 1969 Spain decided to dispel London's illusion that a change of Foreign Minister meant a change in Spanish policy by an act of expressive naval force. The carrier DEDALO and twelve other Spanish warships arrived in the Bay of Algeciras and anchored in sight of the Rock. The British retort was as taciturn and equally traditional, almost blatantly so: when the Armada arrived, a match was being played ashore – between the football teams of HMS EAGLE and HMS HERMES.

DEDALO reappeared in 1970, but it was then still the policy of Her Majesty's Government that 'for most of the year an aircraft carrier, or a commando ship with Royal Marine Commando Groups embarked – will be in the Mediterranean'. In October 1969 DEDALO had actually attracted 10 British warships with 1000 Marines embarked. By 1975 (again quoting the relevant Statement on the Defence Estimates) 'the Government has decided that it cannot in future commit British maritime forces to the Mediterranean'. The Gibraltar garrison, which had been reinforced in 1967, was reduced to an infantry battalion and RAF aircraft were withdrawn from Malta and Cyprus. By 1982 there was one battalion in Gibraltar, no operational aircraft and a destroyer 'on call' (which might mean at Portsmouth).

Although the pattern of the two disputes was so similar, Spain enjoyed important advantages not shared by Argentina. The language of United Nations resolutions on Gibraltar was more peremptory and the backing they received more wide-ranging. In 1967, for instance, the General Assembly not only declared British sovereignty in Gibraltar 'incompatible with the purpose and principles of the Charter of the United Nations', but condemned Britain for holding a referendum to ascertain the wishes of the Gibraltarians. Four members of NATO voted against Britain, seven abstained and only three stood by their Ally. No member of the Common Market backed Britain. These countries not only regarded 'the national unity and territorial integrity' of Spain as menaced by the existence of Gibraltar, but treated the vote of the inhabitants (by 121,338 to 44) for British sovereignty as an impertinent violation of geographical principles. They were also, of course, anxious to retain Spanish goodwill and preserve their military (US bases in Spain) and commercial interests. Spain was better able than Argentina and more inclined than Britain effectively to punish an adverse vote.

Spain's military advantages are even greater. Her army is larger than Britain's and twice the size of Argentina's. Her air force and navy are smaller than Britain's, but she could deploy more and better ships and aircraft against Gibraltar than Argentina could against the Falklands. But Spain's strategic trump is proximity, enabling every arm of the Spanish forces to operate against Gibraltar in optimum conditions. Against serious Spanish attack the fortress of Gibraltar is as indefensible as were the Falkland Islands on 2 April 1982.

This may seem an extreme statement to those who remember how many of its thirteen sieges Gibraltar survived. Unfortunately conditions have changed since Gibraltar emerged triumphantly from the Great (and final) Siege of 1779–83. Then the fortress (garrisoned by 6000 soldiers and over 400 guns) withstood blockade and bombardment from both land and sea for nearly four years, being three times resupplied by a British fleet. Less than a century later the increasing range of artillery made it obvious that guns located out of sight of the fortress could make the harbour unusable. In 1903 it was officially admitted that, failing the occupation of enough of southern Spain to remove all hostile artillery out of range of the harbour, Gibraltar was tenable as a naval base in war only if Spain was neutral.

That condition was met in both World Wars (only just in the Second) and Gibraltar proved a valuable and often an indispensable base for British naval operations in the Mediterranean and in the Atlantic. In neither war, however, was it possible to stop enemy submarines passing the Straits and only the intervention of superior naval forces could prevent transit by surface ships, as the French Navy demonstrated in 1940. Gibraltar was a fortified base for a fleet rather than a fortress capable of controlling the Straits on its own. If the Navy needed the Rock, Gibraltar also needed the Navy. The fall of Singapore in 1942 exemplified the inevitable fate of a distant maritime fortress unsupported by a superior fleet.

Gibraltar's need for naval backing remains, but it is doubtful whether Britain still needs Gibraltar. Withdrawal from Empire, the long closure of the Suez Canal, the development of the super-tanker and the large bulk carrier, the loss of Malta, abstention over Cyprus in 1974, the extinction of the Mediterranean Fleet: all these suggest that the Mediterranean has lost its specifically British importance. With one exception it is hard to envisage any conflict in which Britain would have naval forces to spare for Gibraltar. The exception, of course, is war with Spain: a war fought to retain a superfluous and indefensible fortress.

This was a contingency never examined when the Foreign Affairs Committee of the House of Commons considered the status of Gibraltar in 1980–1. They confirmed and expanded the 1903 verdict:

> now, as in the past, in time of war the use of the dockyard, docks and airfield and of the waters of the Bay would depend upon Spain being in no position to attack or being able either as a neutral or an ally to deny an enemy of Britain the hinterland.[4]

They and the experts called before them preferred to dwell on the value of Gibraltar to NATO. This is dubious. In nuclear war Gibraltar would be as irrelevant as Portsmouth. It is unlikely that general conventional war would last long enough (before escalation or negotiation) for the ability to control passage through the Straits of Gibraltar – which could only be created by the deployment there of substantial forces – to be significant. High level naval war in the Mediterranean would be short and decided by the forces in place at the outset. Only in limited, and correspondingly protracted, war would transit through the Straits matter to either side. Limited Alliance war is quite likely, but it is difficult to envisage the circumstances in which British possession of Gibraltar and willingness to put the base at the disposal of the Alliance would be more important than the Spanish attitude. Spain has more to offer – or to withhold.

It is in violent peace, and to the Super Powers, that the Straits are most important. Maintenance of the Sixth Fleet in the Mediterranean is scarcely possible without unimpeded transit for relief, reinforcement and logistic support. Their most dangerous antagonists – Soviet submarines – are drawn almost entirely from the Northern Fleet and must also pass the Straits, for there are legal and political obstacles to use of the Dardanelles or the Suez Canal. During the 1973 Arab–Israeli War American use of the Straits was crucial for the survival of Israel; Russian for the ability of the Fifth Eskadra to confront the Sixth Fleet. This is a scenario which might be repeated and in which Spanish sympathy for the Arabs might prove as relevant as their opposition to the view that military aircraft may overfly or submarines make a submerged passage of the Straits of Gibraltar. It is far from certain, of course, that either Super Power would be much influenced by the Spanish attitude in a time of crisis. Legally, the status of Gibraltar would not affect the issue, but it is just conceivable that the United States might find Gibraltar a useful base if Spain was unfriendly but not overtly hostile. As the British attitude in the 1973 War was ambiguous, this is not a very convincing argument, but there are some signs that the United States would like to keep such options open. In spite of American abstention in the General Assembly, of the importance long attached to bases in Spain and of the Spanish request of 1968 to refrain from using Gibraltar, US warships have continued to visit Gibraltar. In 1981 a US Navy team even inspected the dockyard. There would nevertheless have to be major political changes before the United States decided to play the British card.

Naturally every argument which depreciates the strategic value to Britain of Gibraltar does the same for Spain. There is no strategic or international or economic purpose which Spain can not pursue without Gibraltar. It does not even command the narrowest part of the Straits. The dispute is entirely sentimental. Only the inhabitants of Gibraltar have a solid stake on the board. Their preference for a continuing autonomy based on British protection and subsidies is understandable, but they would suffer more than anyone else if this choice had to be upheld by force of arms. At best, in the unlikely event of early warning, they could expect to be evacuated, as happened in 1940, to make room for British reinforcements. At worst, they would become the first casualties.

Clearly compromise is desirable. The Spanish proposals of 1966 – base facilities for the British and a special 'personal status' for the Gibraltarians in exchange for Spanish sovereignty – aroused no enthusiasm in either London or Gibraltar. Nor have subsequent events or offers encouraged Gibraltarians to change their mind. The harassment they have suffered; their contemptuous treatment by the Spanish media; the often violent disaffection among Spain's existing minorities; the instability of the Spanish régime and the preponderant influence of the military; these are not the best guarantees of Spanish will and ability to give the Gibraltarians the privileged treatment they have been promised.

Naturally movement is possible. Spain has taken a few small steps to woo the people she has been at such pains to alienate. A handful of Gibraltarian politicians ready to seek accommodation with Spain emerged in 1976. Neither advance has been sustained. The politicians got no seats in the Gibraltar elections of 1980 and the easing of frontier restrictions, offered by Spain in 1980 for 1982, has now been 'indefinitely' suspended. Future progress is likely, at best, to be slow and gradual. Will Spain be content to wait?

The idea that Spain might seize the Rock is usually dismissed on political grounds. Democratic Spain would never do what even Franco shrank from; she would not jeopardise her new-won membership of NATO or her hopes of the Community; she would not risk a real war now that the Falklands have demonstrated Britain's continuing will to make one. These are impressive but uncertain arguments. Spanish democracy is fragile and, even if it prevails, the 29 per cent in favour of military action might be swelled by the 'don't knows' – also 29 per cent. In May 1982 the Spanish Foreign Minister cut Spain's NATO obligations down to size: 'Spain is absolutely not allied to England in the Malvinas.'[5] As he did not need to say, that goes in spades for Gibraltar. Continued membership of the Alliance has also proved compatible with limited conflict between Greece and Turkey, Britain and Iceland.

Future events could, moreover, impart a new twist to present perspectives. A Spanish election might create divisions in Spain for which a spectacular success seemed the only cure. Britain might infuriate every Spaniard by vetoing Spanish entry to the Community. The outcome of a British General Election might radically alter foreign perceptions of British resolution.

Even the Falklands precedent probably seems less conclusive in Spain than it does in Britain. The victory that undid the *fait accompli* Argentina had created was, after all, a near-run thing. If HERMES had been sunk, if INVINCIBLE's engine troubles had proved irremediable at sea, if a dozen other quite conceivable contingencies had occurred, the outcome might have been rather different. What may seem even more persuasive in Spain is the argument that the despatch of a task force to recover Gibraltar after a Spanish *coup de main* would not command the acquiescence, let alone the support, of Britain's Allies. Americans would not jeopardise their Spanish bases, nor Europeans accept a war in their own continent. The pressure applied to Britain to seek a negotiated solution would be of more than Suez dimensions. The interpositioning of the Sixth Fleet might assume a more forceful character than it did in 1956.

Nor would British enthusiasm for a war liable to impinge upon the British Isles necessarily rise to the patriotic heights inspired by a comfortably distant conflict in the Falklands. And even the most robust Ministers might be daunted by the foreseeable requirements of the Chiefs of Staff for such a campaign. A Spanish leader would have much better grounds than General Galtieri for believing that a *fait accompli* could be made to stick.

It would thus be preferable, from every point of view, to create real obstacles to the swift, sure and relatively bloodless seizure of the Rock that is the only military option likely to receive serious Spanish consideration. Even a short siege would mean that Spain would suffer, and Britain escape, the Allied pressures previously described. In the eyes of what passes for international opinion, possession is nine points of the law and local resistance as acceptable as counter-attack is aggressive.

Sir Robert Gardiner knew what he was talking about when he envisaged Spain 'repossessing Gibraltar' by 'stratagem' and Barry Wynne provided a plausible scenario in 1969: a surprise night attack by infiltrated 'tourists', assisted by frogmen and small boat landings, to disarm defences and prepare for the arrival at dawn of paratroops and armour.[6] What is needed is an increased garrison (with a larger Gibraltarian contribution); modernised fixed defences; more resources and effort for security, surveillance and intelligence; and a real naval presence. Not a destroyer 'on call', but INVINCIBLE, FEARLESS (with commandos embarked) and escorts based on Gibraltar and visibly cruising in the vicinity. Not to resist a siege, a bombardment, a divisional assault: merely to ensure that Gibraltar can not be captured without a war. Nobody wants a war.

If a renewal of British maritime presence in the Western Mediterranean, a halt to naval cuts, even an increase in naval strength, are unacceptable, then the Gibraltarians should be advised to come to terms with Spain.

Since 2 April 1982 'It may never happen' is no longer an admissible reply. To maintain British sovereignty over disputed territory without taking precautions against the obvious threat would be unfair to the Gibraltarians – even to Spain. To expect the Royal Navy, or the rest of the armed forces, or the British people, to remedy the predictable consequences of this ostrich policy would be outrageous. It might also prove, the Falklands precedent notwithstanding, to be impossible. It is thus today, and in London, that a decisive answer is needed to the initial question: will Gibraltar be next?

5 Diplomacy: a Case for Resuscitation

DIPLOMACY CONTRASTED WITH POLICY FORMATION

Diplomacy is a word as much misunderstood as it is widely abused. Its extensions, variant meanings and misapplications would furnish too much matter for a thesis and could only be comfortably accommodated, perhaps in association with 'love' and 'democracy', in a supplement to the *Oxford English Dictionary*. In the restricted space of an essay the field of dispute must be arbitrarily and drastically narrowed.

Even the definition which Harold Nicolson adapted[1] from an earlier edition of that great dictionary must be sharpened to focus the attention of the reader on a single aspect of a controversy as diffuse as it is impassioned.

Diplomacy is the method by which international relations are adjusted and managed by ambassadors and envoys.

Diplomacy, therefore, is a process. As such it must first be distinguished from a kindred process: the formation of foreign policy.

Policy formation embraces a wide range of very diverse activities. Few of them are either rational or deliberate. Some of them are doubtfully conscious. There is, for instance, the almost biological emergence, evolution, modification and transformation of the assumptions, attitudes and preconceptions that express a nation's idea of its own standing and purpose in the world. The nature of this process has received as many interpretations as there are theorists, but we need only note the outcome: the creation of a framework for conscious decisions. This framework is neither rigid nor clear-cut, it is a misty and shifting horizon, difficult to discern and impossible to measure. But, for policy-makers, it indicates the uncertain limits of the possible and the clouded extent of the desirable. Beyond it lie the unseen but real perils of the commanding negative, whether expressed in popular resistance or in resource constraints.

The conscious component of policy-formation, the tip of the iceberg, is usually dominated by a few broad concepts intended to crystallise the attitudes derived from the unconscious base and from the external environment. These may be very general: the priority accorded by present British policy to 'interdependence'; by Finnish to the delicate balance between national independence and Soviet tolerance; by the Arabs to the reconciliation of national development with the doctrine of *'delenda est Israel'*. They may be addressed to relations with a particular country or to a single problem: Indian attitudes towards Pakistan or Spanish claims to Gibraltar. Their essential characteristics are that they are internally generated, remain valid for years rather than months and serve as yardsticks, however rough and flexible, for more specific decisions.

These last, though of very varying intrinsic importance, constitute the major component of conscious policy-formation by virtue of their cumulative influence. They are numerous, often hasty, usually reactive, sometimes mutually conflicting. They provide the case-law of foreign policy and the catalyst of its continuous transmutation.

This is a logical rather than a descriptive dissection of policy-formation. There is not nothing sequential about the actual process. All its elements are in simultaneous evolution and constant interaction. The argument for choosing this perspective is that it makes it easier to relate the nature of the process to participation in the process. With large variations from one country and one era to another, participation tends to diminish as the process becomes less general and more specific; less concerned with abstract principles and more with concrete problems; less enduring and more immediate; less negative and more initiatory. There are few countries in which a small group can not by themselves take single decisions, however momentous: Britain over Suez in 1956 or the United States in the Cuban Missile crisis of 1962. There are fewer still in which a wide-ranging policy requiring years of consistent application can be successfully prosecuted without at least popular acquiescence.

This pattern of diminishing participation in policy-formation is domestic. Foreign participation follows an opposite trend, exercising most influence on particular decisions, least on general attitudes. In Britain, for instance, incoming Ministers, flushed by electoral endorsement of the principles they have propounded on the hustings, soon become aware of the existence of a watershed in the process of policy-formation. This occurs at the point where domestic preconceptions have to yield place to foreign reactions as the dominant influence.

Between the idea
And the reality
Between the motion
And the act
Falls the Shadow.[2]

INTERFUSION AND CONFUSION OF THE TWO PROCESSES

Some politicians and many of their ideologically more committed supporters, particularly, but not exclusively in insular Britain, are apt to identify that Shadow with Diplomacy. Attributing to the messenger the news he bears they sometimes regard their professional advisers as the agents of their frustration. Even civil servants unversed in foreign affairs often envisage the Foreign Office as a Department no less committed to the interests of foreigners than is the Ministry of Agriculture to those of farmers.

The fallacies of this view need not be argued here. What matters is the reality it conceals. Diplomats, whether serving at home or abroad, do contribute to policy-formation. This is inevitable. Foreign policy is:

> that general conception of national aspirations, interests and capacities which influences the Government in the identification of disputes with other governments and in the choice of methods for the prevention, determination or limitation of such disputes.[3]

No such general conception will be fruitful without an informed understanding of the foreign attitudes likely to occasion disputes. A foreign policy unconditioned by the international environment is purpose operating in a vacuum, which does not exist. Foreigners do: another of those facts of life which have to experienced to be appreciated.

This experience of foreigners is an indispensable part of the 'method by which international relations are adjusted and managed by ambassadors and envoys': diplomacy. To many this will be an unwelcome, indeed a controversial view. At this stage of the argument it will be enough to note an inconvenient side-effect. It blurs the desirable distinction between policy-formation and diplomacy. It would be tidier if a line could be drawn between the domestic process of taking a decision and the international process of seeking to implement that decision through discussion with foreigners. This was a distinction sought by Harold Nicolson and he further balanced his picture by assigning the first task to responsible leaders at home and the second to ambassadors and envoys abroad.

In the real world such symmetry is threatened from both directions. Not only do diplomats aspire to influence policy, but those at home who take decisions are also eager to extol their merits to foreigners. Neither tendency is new, but each is growing.

The notion that a Foreign Minister takes a decision and an Ambassador implements it has always been subject to exceptions. Talleyrand combined both functions at the Congress of Vienna in 1814. So did Castlereagh, for that matter. Nor was this the last nineteenth-century meeting at which Foreign Ministers, even Heads of State, acted as genuine plenipotentiaries. In the twentieth century the pace has quickened, but the rôle of the foreign-based plenipotentiary has declined. In 1854 Lord Stratford de Redcliffe, as Ambassador at Constantinople, imposed a policy on his own government. His subsequent claim that the Crimean War was 'my war' has, at least in part, been endorsed by later historians. The speed of modern communications makes it almost inconceivable that his feat could be emulated today.

On the other hand, the number of home-based officials authorised to enter into international commitments has greatly increased. The decisions they take, admittedly, are usually of no great intrinsic importance, but policy is, as already argued, in large part the aggregation of innumerable minor decisions. The officials for ever shuttling to and fro between London and Brussels are building, brick by little brick, a structure of precedent and commitment which British governments may later find it difficult to demolish or alter. The history of the Common Fisheries Policy of the European Economic Community is a case in point.

DECLINING COORDINATION AND CONTROL

The existence of numerous officials from the Foreign Office and, still more so, from other Departments, who deal direct with their opposite numbers abroad, whether in personal meetings or on the telephone, has far-reaching implications. It does not only mean that the British Government speak to foreigners with many more different voices. It also tends to the fragmentation of policy and the erosion of ministerial, let alone parliamentary control over that policy. These are, of course, tendencies that have been gathering force all this century. The proportion of communications to foreigners enjoying prior ministerial sanction, or even cognisance, has diminished at a vertiginous rate as the volume of international transactions has exploded. For a long time, however, a rudimentary check was preserved. Communications to foreigners were authorised in writing by the Foreign Office, increasingly in the form of telegrams. These telegrams, often originated by very junior officials, were promptly and widely circulated. Anyone transcending the bounds of accepted policy or allowing a particular objective to prejudice wider purposes could expect instant enquiry and rebuke, even in the red ink sacred to the Secretary of State. This was an effective deterrent to those individual initiatives to which the most dedicated officials are also the most susceptible. Nowadays it is much harder for any minister to be sure what has been conceded, whether over a convivial luncheon in Brussels or in a telephone call, by some civil servant preoccupied by a particular aspect of what he regards as domestic policy.

Two anecdotes may serve to illustrate the extent of this largely unperceived revolution. Quarter of a century ago an Under-Secretary in the Foreign Office had just returned from a visit to Paris. He instructed one of his subordinates to telephone a member of the Quai d'Orsay to confirm a point not resolved in their discussions. A few hours later the Minister of the Paris Embassy was on the telephone to voice an indignant protest at a communication, however trivial, that had bypassed the Embassy. The Under-Secretary was so abashed that he unscrupulously laid the entire blame on his subordinate.

The transference of odium to one's staff is, unfortunately, still a favourite gambit of the ambitious in every profession. The point is that, today, there would be no odium. The right to discuss specialised subjects with foreigners is widely disseminated.

This is not something that happens only within the Community. In 1976 it was reasonable to write:

> The distinctively European phenomenon of the displacement of diplomatic intermediaries by direct exchanges between responsible officials from national capitals has posed far more acutely for them [Members of the EEC] the problem of maintaining coherence and coordination over foreign policy as a whole.[4]

In 1983 one may legitimately query two of those epithets: 'distinctively' and 'responsible'.

A few years ago, for instance, there arrived in the capital of a country outside the Community a group of British civil servants. Their presence was discovered by alert members of the Embassy and they were invited to drinks by the Ambassador. Thus mellowed, they disclosed their intention of announcing to the foreign officials concerned the imposition of certain restrictions on exports to Britain. When it was explained that this would prejudice the negotiation of a much more important and hotly contested order for British aircraft, they readily agreed to depart from their instructions. The original incompatibility was not their fault: they had never heard of the aircraft order that had preoccupied the Embassy and other Departments in London for years; their horizon was bounded by a single commodity.

Most British Embassies, unless situated in countries with intolerable climates and indifferent hotels, could recount more disconcerting stories – without the happy ending. What seems in Whitehall a minor decision taken on its technical merits may be perceived by foreigners as the last straw confirming a diagnosis of British policy towards their country as generally either unfriendly or appeasing or untrustworthy. Allowing civil servants, legitimately preoccupied by the particular and predominantly domestic problems entrusted to their care, plenipotentiary rights of communication with foreigners is inevitably destructive both of the unity of foreign policy and of ministerial responsibility.

This is a problem often more acute in other capitals than Brussels, where the presence of a powerful permanent delegation in intimate contact with the network of interdepartmental committees in London achieves greater coordination of British policies towards the Community than might be expected.

These are aspects of the hydra-headed conduct of Britain's international business which have received curiously little attention. The CPRS report of 1977, for instance, strongly advocated reliance on visits from home-based officials. It did so on two grounds. The first, which will require further examination at a later stage of the argument, was that: 'The expertise required is expertise in the subject matter more than expertise in living among and working with foreigners.'[5] The second was a statistically elaborate, but specious calculation that this would be cheaper. Much effort was devoted to comparing the cost of the man-hours spent on visits to foreign capitals with that of maintaining resident representatives in those capitals. No figures were given for the total number of those thus authorised to travel abroad and communicate with foreigners, nor for the proportion of working time devoted to these touristic activities. The report did mention, however, that officials of the Department of Trade and Industry had made 3528 visits abroad in 1975.[6] That was one of a dozen Departments with international interests. Making reasonable allowance for subsequent proliferation, it is a conservative assumption that there are today many hundreds of civil servants authorised to leave London and commit the British Government abroad.

Who are they? The staff of every British diplomatic mission or consulate is listed in a dozen reference books. The Head of that Mission is personally responsible for every transaction by his subordinates. Only the insiders know which home-based officials talk to foreigners and on what subjects. Even the nomenclature and composition of the Whitehall committees coordinating European and other international business are treated as secret – unlike the organisation and staffing of the Foreign Office. Dr David Owen, then Foreign Secretary, had a legitimate point when he told the House of Commons Committee considering the CPRS report: 'One of the problems in Britain is that there are not enough people who are named and hold responsibility.'[7]

Whatever else may result from the proliferation of anonymous negotiators, one consequence is certain: the loss of democratic control. Parliament may legitimately, and frequently does, hold the Foreign Secretary responsible for the errors of ambassadors. Some of those ambassadors have even had uncomfortable cause to regard the House of Commons as the only audience attentive to their after-dinner speeches. But which Minister even knows of the repercussions of some casual transaction concerning apples or steel quotas or the standardisation of tank treads? Today the experts are no longer on tap: they are on top.

PERIPATETIC DIPLOMACY

No such constitutional issues are raised by the ever-increasing frequency with which Ministers travel abroad to conduct negotiations or hold discussions. As elected representatives, members of the government, directly responsible to Parliament, they have a better right than most, subject to any restrictions the Prime Minister or the Foreign Secretary may impose, to commit their colleagues. The publicity usually attending their travels makes unauthorised initiatives unlikely and the evasion of responsibility difficult.

There are, however, two practical problems, both deriving from the extreme pressures on the time and attention of contemporary ministers, particularly those of senior rank.

The first problem is that they have to negotiate in exceptionally unfavourable circumstances. Their normal duties at home leave them little leisure for mastering their briefs (often an inch or two thick), which must accordingly be perused in the aircraft or even in the car taking them to their first meeting. They are thus liable to arrive less well prepared than their adversary, who will, in any case, have avoided the inevitable fatigue and disruption of travel. In the foreign capital their stay will be brief, its duration usually limited by other commitments at home. It may nevertheless be further curtailed by a sudden summons to return for an unexpected division in the House of Commons. This happens with surprising frequency, even to the most important visitors, when the government's majority is slender or precarious. In many countries their programme will also include banquets, entertainments, formal calls and even sight-seeing, all activities which a visiting minister, particularly if he is coming for the first time, may be unable to refuse without causing offence. The climate and food are often sufficiently unfamiliar to strain the visitor's metabolism and reduce his stamina. None of these disadvantages is suffered by a resident ambassador, who can concentrate his efforts on the task in hand.

Nor is the ambassador under any personal time pressure. He does not have to be back in London on Wednesday. He can, if this seems tactically desirable, stall, spin out the negotiations, plead the necessity to refer home for further instructions. He does not need an early, if illusory, triumph to announce to the press and, if disagreement seems preferable to concession, his reputation will not suffer.

Nowhere are these contrasts more evident than in Moscow. The Minister arrives with a numerous retinue, for no ambitious official cares to admit that his presence could be superfluous on such occasions. All carry large boxes covered in scarlet leather and stuffed with documents. These they open beneath the ambiguous ceiling of the large conference room on the seventh floor of the Soviet Foreign Ministry. They must be ready to advise and inform their Minister, as the author once told a Soviet official who had poked fun at the array of red boxes. He laughed 'We never have to advise Mr Gromyko: he knows it all.'

So he should. More than forty years have passed since he was first appointed Ambassador in Washington, all of them devoted to the conduct of international relations, half of them as Foreign Minister. Unencumbered by parliamentary responsibilities, with no worries about the media or the opposition, seldom submitting to the fatigue of foreign travel, he is the player confronting courtesy gentlemen. Not all his colleagues are equally accomplished, but there are few capitals in which the arrival of a ministerial delegation, even if it is not British, excites more apprehension among the resident diplomats than it does in Moscow. Which is not, when all is said and done, an unimportant capital.

This is not a factor to be exaggerated. Most ministerial trips abroad are in fact, as they are in intention, of greater domestic than international significance. In the few cases where important business must be transacted, it is nevertheless worth remembering that the itinerant envoy needs exceptional personal advantages to overcome the handicaps imposed by his touristic status.

THE IMPACT ON POLICY-FORMATION

A much more important consideration is what is happening at home while the decision-makers are abroad. Perhaps Lord Carrington was merely unlucky that Argentina invaded the Falklands while he was visiting Israel. But the coincidence emphasises a serious issue. In the past, when a British Foreign Secretary travelled abroad, he resigned the care of the Foreign Office to one of his colleagues. Nowadays, so we are assured, the marvels of modern communications enable the responsible Minister to discharge his duties wherever he is. That was the view taken by Dr Kissinger, when he was touring the Middle East, or by General Haig, when he was shuttling in quest of a peaceful solution to the Falklands crisis.

This notion has some merit when the journey is long and its purpose primarily representational. The seclusion of the chartered aircraft may then provide a welcome opportunity to catch up with the paper-work. It is a different matter when arduous negotiations or even crisis await the traveller at his destination. There is then little of the overburdened day left for thinking about anything but the matter in hand. The Private Secretary must reluctantly trespass on his master's brief moments of relaxation to squeeze quarter of an hour for the telegrams demanding decisions on the rest of the world's problems.

Naturally many decisions can be taken by the junior ministers and senior officials left in London, though these, too, have their travelling schedules. In the Foreign Office itself the main result is further exaggeration of the habitual tendency to concentrate on immediate decisions at the expense of future problems or wider trends. The office meeting at which these were to have been discussed is, first repeatedly then indefinitely, postponed. Some hard-pressed Foreign Secretaries have proved understandably reluctant to see anyone, British or foreign, who did not have urgent business to transact. Even Under-Secretaries found access difficult if they dealt with countries or problems momentarily quiescent. Many ambassadors, British or foreign, seldom met the Secretary of State.

The main casualty was the conscious, deliberate element of policy-formation. But there were also diplomatic side-effects. Foreigners, particularly representatives or visitors from countries outside the Central Triangle of Europe, United States, Soviet Union, resented the denial of a personal contact more readily available elsewhere, even in Moscow. British ambassadors, always expected to secure access to Head of State or Government for junior British Ministers or important members of parliament visiting a foreign capital, were handicapped by their inability to secure reciprocal courtesies for foreign visitors to London.

In 1975 Mr Callaghan, then Foreign Secretary, was abroad for ninety-five days.[8] When allowance is made for the machine-gun rhythm of the daily telegrams, for his domestic responsibilities – in the Cabinet, in the House of Commons, to his constituency, to his Party – and for his insufficient but indispensable days of rest and relaxation, he can scarcely have been more than a part-time maker of foreign policy. To a lesser extent the same was true of many of his subordinates, whose proposals could, in any case, only bear fruit if they could catch the ear of the Secretary of State. Something had to be sacrificed to this unrelenting pressure. It has usually been, for at least thirty years, those problems which seemed difficult, complex and important – but not urgent.

In other Departments the consequences were less momentous, but actually more acute. The Foreign Office, after all, are organised and staffed for the conduct of international relations. Under the new pressures of foreign travel their decisions might be ill-considered, but they remained prompt. Elsewhere the small section dealing with international affairs might be paralysed by the absence abroad of a couple of officials. British Embassies found it increasingly difficult to obtain quick decisions, or even replies, from, for instance, the Department of Trade.

Although stated largely in terms of British experience, the fundamental problem is one that is common to many countries today. It is particularly acute for those governments committed to constant discussion of a wide range of practical business in such multilateral organisations as the European Economic Community or the North Atlantic Treaty Organisation. British Foreign Secretaries are not alone in allotting over 10 per cent of their time to such meetings. It is important for the larger number of governments whose domestic policies are partly dependent on international agreement concerning finance, trade, aid, agriculture, civil aviation and the like. But it also affects those more traditional preoccupations of foreign policy: 'peace, war, neutrality and alliance or various combinations of or approaches to these'.[9] It has become increasingly fashionable to tackle such problems by loading a Foreign Minister, even a Head of Government or Head of State, onto an aircraft bound for some distant destination. This practice is not without its dangers for those concerned. Prince Sihanouk and President Nkrumah were only the most notable of the many statesmen whose diplomatic missions turned out to have been undertaken on a one-way ticket: a possible explanation of the vehemence with which Mr Foot, that indefatigable travel agent, urged British Ministers to visit the Americas at the outset of the Falklands crisis.

The risk of a *coup d'état* in one's absence is nevertheless only a special case of a more general objection. What happens to policy, great or small, general or particular, while its maker is absorbed by itinerant diplomacy?

Enough has already been said to suggest one word as the answer: neglect. The handicaps suffered by the itinerant envoy need no further emphasis. One question remains. Are there such advantages in despatching a special emissary from the capital that these outweigh all the penalties? Or must the prevalence of this custom be ascribed to other factors?

ARGUMENTS FOR EMISSARIES

There are certain situations in which the despatch of special envoys is generally advocated.

The first category is essentially that of crisis. The issues may seem too important or too pressing to be entrusted to a resident ambassador. If it is a question of war or peace; when major concessions must be made; when fundamental changes in policy are contemplated: there is often a case for letting the responsible Minister negotiate the decision he must take. Chamberlain's journeys to Berchtesgaden, to Bad Godesberg and to Munich were necessary to stamp his concessions with his personal authority and thus to make them acceptable at home. Attlee's visit to Truman during the Korean War made more impact, both in Washington and in London, than representations from an ambassador. What matters is not negotiating skill but public emphasis of the importance attached to the negotiations.

Not all crises respond to such treatment and in many the risk exists that the despatch of a senior minister will be perceived as a sign of weakness. The present British Government were wise to resist Mr Foot's importunity and to ration ministerial travel during the Falklands crisis. Sometimes, however, such journeys are useful and they will usually be demanded by public opinion. Significantly, French being the traditional language of diplomacy, the accepted translation of 'scapegoat' is 'bouc émissaire'.

The case is stronger when the requirement is for mediation in a multilateral crisis. The problems created by Israeli invasion of the Lebanon in 1982, for instance, could scarcely have been tackled by the bilateral representations, however well coordinated, of resident ambassadors. Mr Habib's journey was necessary and, as he was not a minister, carried fewer penalties in terms of American policy-formation. Even the earlier excursions of Dr Kissinger or, in the Rhodesian dispute, of Lord Carrington brought more rewards than penalties. If failure is more frequent than success – Robert Kennedy's attempt to resolve Britain's Confrontation with Indonesia by a South-East Asian tour was particularly disastrous – the same is true of all diplomatic expedients.

In a crisis the employment of special envoys is nowadays as usual as other extraordinary means of communication: the hot line, personal messages, broadcasts and public statements, ostentatious military precautions and organised incidents of violence. Any of these may be useful in some circumstances, but they all have the disadvantage of raising the temperature of the crisis. Sometimes, of course, this is the object of the exercise. But the employment of special envoys carries an extra penalty if they are also policy-makers, for what their journey adds to negotiations abroad must often be subtracted from decisions at home.

A different category comprises those issues considered too complex or too technical for negotiation otherwise then among experts. Here a distinction must be made between consensus negotiations and adversary negotiations. If the principles are agreed and only the details have to be settled; if a give and take of commitments across the table is likely; if the subject is narrow and the time allotted for its discussion is brief: then there is much to be said for sending out an expert – if he really is an expert and not just a generalist civil servant newly seconded to the Ministry of Agriculture. Adversary negotiations, particularly those in which the issues, however technical, have wider implications; which are likely to be protracted and to involve frequent reference home for confirmation or further instructions: these are another matter. Such issues are not decided on their technical merits. Moreover, when the time is available, the extra effort needed to explain technical arguments to one's own diplomats usually results in the presentation of a better case to the adversary. British representation at the Vienna talks on Mutual and Balanced Force Reductions in Central Europe, for instance, has rightly been entrusted to a resident ambassador, even if he is assisted by expert advisers.

A more impressive argument for the itinerant negotiator can be derived from the special case of the European Economic Community. Here, so it is often contended, much of the business transacted does not concern foreign policy at all, but is merely an extension of various domestic policies. William Wallace goes even further

> foreign policy has ceased to be a discrete field – it would be more appropriate to talk about a foreign policy dimension across the whole range of domestic politics, demanding particular attention from particular ministers, civil servants and commentators, but inseparable from the major issues of domestic debate.[10]

It is scarcely surprising that people imbued with such ideas should extend them by questioning the need for diplomacy, let alone for a diplomatic service.

The logic is seductive and has been widely deployed, with the aid of much statistical apparatus, in recent years. It is nevertheless important to remember that it springs, as did Cobden's favourite toast, over a century ago, of 'no foreign politics', from political preconceptions of a rather special kind. These were most obvious and most extreme in the CPRS report,[11] but Wallace's comment has a wider application:

> The idea that foreign policy is separate from domestic policy is fundamental to the traditional concept of the nation-state – over the last century in British politics this has usually been accepted by all sides excepting the dissenting minority of the radical left.[12]

Much may be deduced from the premise that the nation-state is obsolescent and the national interest an unreal concept, but a different starting-point imposes altogether different conclusions. Political developments since Wallace's book appeared in 1975, or the CPRS report in 1977, scarcely suggest general acceptance, either in Britain or in other countries, of the death of the nation-state.

The most compelling, widespread and persistent reason for the tourism of ministers and home-based officials is nevertheless neither conceptual nor practical. It is simply a matter of 'keeping up with the Joneses'. If a meeting is to be attended by other Foreign Ministers, it is rude not to send one's own. If one country fields a general, two scientists and a leading industrialist for forthcoming talks, they ought to be matched. Ambassadors feel guilty of discourtesy, are even conscious of diminished prestige, if the capital where they reside has attracted fewer distinguished delegations from their own country than from others. Only a special journey will do for funerals, centenaries, declarations of independence and the installation of important presidents. In all these respects the author must confess himself as guilty as anyone else. Nor was he alone in hoping that it might be professionally rewarding to extol the advantages to be expected from a personal visit from London. In one case he was partly right: the visit provided the only meeting, in five years as a British Ambassador, with a British Foreign Secretary.

These are factors that nothing but a change in fashion will overcome. It is irrelevant that the results of such visits are usually nugatory when they are not negative. The public do not realise that, when the Foreign Secretary and his extensive entourage step into their chartered VC 10, the communiqué announcing the result of his momentous discussions has already been drafted, often even discussed with officials of the country concerned. They are content that their affairs are being treated seriously and at the highest level. The more numerous visits of junior ministers and mere officials seldom get into the British papers, but are more extensively reported abroad. British Embassies scrutinise these reports with great care, send a prudent selection (including all the presentable photographs) to London and apply themselves to repairing the damage.

IS THERE AN ALTERNATIVE?

Today, therefore, the conduct of diplomacy is both widely diffused and considerably entangled with the separate, if kindred process of forming foreign policy. The results have not always been regrettable: further exceptions could easily be added to those already mentioned. On the whole, however, the rewards of this blurring of functions have been outweighed by the penalties: the sacrifice by policy-makers of the important to the urgent; less thought and more talk; the fragmentation of policy and of its presentation to foreigners; the loss of democratic control as decision-takers have become more numerous and more anonymous; negotiation at an inherent disadvantage; one person trying to do two jobs.

Four questions remain. Is the degrading of diplomacy an inevitable trend, just one of those changes which the second half of the twentieth century has brought to every aspect of international relations and social organisation? Or is a different approach still possible? If so, would this be applicable to all governmental transactions involving foreigners or can these be divided into separate categories requiring distinctive techniques? Finally, to quote William Wallace, 'what do we need our structure of overseas representation for?'[13]

In answer to the first question it is hard to avoid a gloomy determinism. So much has altered in the last twenty-five years and so seldom for the better, that diplomacy can scarcely expect to escape the general *dégringolade*. Two arguments, of unequal importance, nevertheless offer crumbs of comfort to the traditionalist. The first is the existence of that great conservative power, the Soviet Union. As long as the Russians are reluctant to send their leaders abroad, anxious to restrict travel by their officials and attach obvious importance to resident ambassadors – Dobrynin has been in Washington since 1962 – it will be difficult for lesser countries to neglect the traditional methods preferred by a Super Power. The second is that Britain is one of several countries with a government trying to reverse trends that, only a decade ago, were regarded as definitively established. The choice of targets has not so far included diplomacy and the objectives do not command universal approval, but putting the clock back has returned to the realm of the politically possible.

It is uncertain whether as much can be said for the true alternative to the present confusion: reliance on professional intermediaries to analyse foreign attitudes, to communicate with foreigners and to negotiate with foreigners. The case for it rests on such heretical propositions as: foreigners exist; they have their own interests, aspirations and assumptions; these are different from ours; the choice between coercion, compromise and concession is more satisfactorily resolved if foreign views are understood than if they are ignored. Even worse: foreigners must be studied in their natural habitat before they can be understood.

This obviously brings us back to the argument advanced by the CPRS report: 'the expertise required is expertise in the subject matter more than expertise in living among and working with foreigners.'[14] Let us consider a few examples. Lamb has been a long-standing subject of dispute between Britain and France. Could this best be resolved by sheep-farmers and butchers (if there are any in the Ministry of Agriculture) or should the internal politics, economy and social conditions of France, to say nothing of wider French policies, French psychology and the general relationship between Britain and France, be regarded as more relevant? And who knows most about them? Britain has differences with her Community partners over the budget and the Common Fisheries Policy. Are these technical or political? What expertise, in which subject matter, was needed to resolve the Falklands crisis or to prevent similar problems arising over Belize, Diego Garcia, Gibraltar or Hong Kong?

Knowledge of the subject matter is important when the misunderstanding of technical details seems the only obstacle to agreement, when, in short, there is no dispute.

Is this a pointer to compromise: reserving for foreign policy and diplomacy the contentious aspects of relations with other countries, while allowing the home-based a free run of the rest? Compromise, after all, there must be. Too many people have tasted the pleasures of foreign travel on short-stay package tours ever to accept relegation to Whitehall. It would be as much a come-down as a holiday at Blackpool. Conceptually the case is arguable. In principle much of the work of the European Economic Community is concerned with harmonisation, where the only adversary is the ordinary citizen. In practice the distinction would be difficult to maintain: there is no subject which never generates disputes between close friends. Moreover, relations between two countries are governed by much the same principle as minor motoring offences: the smallest and most technical of grievances are liable to be totted up. But it would be much more invidious to withdraw a negotiating licence from a Home Department than it is to send a ministerial delegation to some foreign capital when a dispute gets into the papers.

However reluctantly, it must be admitted that there is only one clear dividing line: between business that concerns foreigners and business that does not. The hopes, or fears, of the early seventies that the

European Economic Community would acquire a supranational character in which the divisions would be functional, even political, rather than national, stand out clearly, in 1983, as illusions. There is, at most, *une Europe des Patries*, and even that is still a matter of political controversy in Britain. Interdependence is a transitory dogma: as important, as persuasive, perhaps as durable as The Protestant Cause, Maritime Supremacy, The Balance of Power, but no more. Such slogans come and go. The national interest remains. So do foreigners.

The true problem is not how to divide responsibility in this field, but how to unify it: to coordinate both policy and its implementation.

The solution offered by the CPRS report was to dismantle everything that existed and to create a new structure, to be called a Foreign Service Group, of which the disparate elements would be controlled by a network of interdepartmental committees. The snags are obvious, but one has received insufficient attention. No single Minister would be responsible to Parliament or the electorate. Even those who most regretted the resignation of Lord Carrington would not deny that his conduct was honourable, as much admired abroad as at home and conducive to a proper sense of responsibility in future. Committees are as conscienceless as they are unaccountable.

A better alternative would be to absorb into the Foreign Office those sections of other Departments with international responsibilities, to expand the Diplomatic Service by the inclusion of officials with appropriate experience or skills and to make the Foreign Secretary, advised, assisted and even controlled by his cabinet colleagues, responsible for the entire direction of Britain's external relations.

In practice, of course, neither alternative will be adopted. Nor will any rational or deliberate compromise emerge. Britain will continue to muddle the conduct of her external relations and some optimism will be required to support the belief that she will muddle through.

PRESERVING THE OPTION OF DIPLOMACY

It would be wishful thinking to advocate a full return to a practice always subject to exceptions: the adjustment and management of international relations by ambassadors and envoys. It would be still more foolish to renounce all possibility of greater resort to an expedient which has often proved useful in the past and which still retains great potential for the future. Retention of this option, however, demands the preservation of a structure of overseas representation.

Although some of the advantages of overseas representation have emerged as fleeting reflections of the criticisms levelled at the alternatives to diplomacy, these fragments of a shattered mirror must now be assembled into a more coherent argument. Resident ambassadors abroad are needed for the following reasons.

First, and most important, they can enlighten their own government on the nature of foreign attitudes. Secondly, they can continuously disseminate among foreigners knowledge of the attitudes of their own government. Thirdly, they can negotiate with foreigners discreetly and without creating tension by their mere presence, with greater understanding of the adversary and without assuming the stance of the advocate who argues his own cause and notoriously has a fool as a client. Finally, their comprehensive and nowadays often unique grasp of the totality of British relations with the country to which they are accredited can prevent many errors otherwise unavoidable.

The value of these tasks is seldom contested. Instead the critics maintain that they could be discharged at less expense by others.

It is often suggested, for instance, that reciprocal communication of different national attitudes can safely be left to the media and satisfactorily supplemented by the fleeting impressions gained by visitors from capitals.

Naturally the media, with their extensive network of correspondents abroad, could provide much of the information supplied by ambassadors in major capitals. They do not do so, because it is not their job. The business of the media is entertainment: sensational events, scandal, wit and colour to suit the editor's taste and, of course, statistics for the investor. A continuous analysis of those foreign attitudes relevant to British interests and policies would have even less audience appeal than a party political broadcast. Nor are the media concerned to disseminate abroad the views of the British Government. Anyone who, in April 1982, relied on the British press and television as an indicator of British intentions must have had a rude awakening. Perhaps General Galtieri did.

As for the impressions of visitors, we need only recall Chamberlain's of Hitler or Roosevelt's of Stalin.[15]

Similar scrutiny of other alternatives to diplomacy would be superfluous, for such expedients are seldom suggested from any conviction of their intrinsic merits. Alternatives are sought because diplomacy is distrusted. This is a feeling deeply rooted in the traditional folk-lore of radical dissent, which sees diplomats both as agents of the ruling class and as professionally interested in fomenting the very disputes among nations which they are supposed to moderate. Few of the critics, perhaps, would seriously argue that the abolition of diplomats would eliminate disputes – as if one were to remove from a nuclear reactor the expensive and unproductive graphite that encumbers it – but the instinct is there. Curiously enough it is matched by an opposite prejudice of different origins: that a compulsive itch to conciliate prevents diplomats from ever prosecuting disputes with the vigour to be expected from soldiers, successful businessmen or popular politicians.

These deep under-currents of the collective subconscious merge in resentment of the large houses occupied by ambassadors, the deference shown to them, those notorious entertainment allowances, the higher standard of living and the general atmosphere of privilege that surrounds diplomacy. There is quite a widespread feeling that such advantages should be reserved for pop stars, whereas ambassadors could perfectly well live in a small flat and discharge their duties at a desk or by visiting ministers and officials in their offices.

This sentiment is probably ineradicable, for it springs from the envy natural to human beings. It also reflects the routine familiar to the average office worker. Young men and women accustomed to bureaucratic seclusion are often disconcerted, even shocked, to be told, on arrival at their first post overseas, that every hour a diplomat spends at his desk is an hour wasted, one in which he is learning nothing and influencing nobody.

The problem facing the ambassador can only be appreciated by understanding what he really is. Whatever his social origin, education or personal characteristics, in the country to which he is accredited he is an undesirable alien.

In many countries he is openly regarded as a spy and a subversive influence. Everywhere he is the agent of a foreign power, one who will try to find out more than official statements reveal, but who will constrain his own utterances to fit the policies of his government. Although his trade makes him an inquisitive bore, it seldom allows him to reward those he pesters. He does not pay them for taking up their time, hand out contracts or offer advantageous publicity. He is simply a nuisance.

There are various ways of overcoming this handicap. The ambassador may represent a government so important to the host country –

the Soviet Ambassador in Finland, for instance – that all its inhabitants will strive to please him. A Portuguese Ambassador once
achieved an unique position as the only person always willing to
partner King Edward VII at bridge. A modern ambassador may be
endowed with such personal charm and magnetism that everybody
wants to meet him and falls under his spell. These expedients are not
generally available and the last is much rarer than some ambassadors
believe.

The ordinary ambassador belongs to the overwhelming majority
and needs artificial aids to escape from the deformities imposed by his
profession.

The first of these aids is the glamour, not of his person, but of his
position, which persuades many people with no obligation to receive an
ambassador actually to welcome his visits. Glamour is an artefact of
custom and of the media, particularly the latter. The staunchest of
suburban Tories, who would shut his door in the face of an anonymous Labour canvasser, might invite Mr Benn in for a cup of tea. The
ambassador's glamour is assisted by the big house and the conspicuous car, but is largely created by the ability to dispense hospitality (not
least to the media) in agreeable surroundings. Even in Communist
countries, where special permission must be obtained to accept
ambassadorial invitations, these are sought, as they are elsewhere, by
people who would never dream of visiting the Chancery.

This generalised hospitality gives the ambassador his aura as
someone ordinary people would like to meet and usefully widens his
acquaintance. Specialised hospitality is more important. There are few
countries nowadays in which ministers, politicians, generals, business
tycoons, officials, editors, trade union leaders and the like are not
very busy people. Their days are overburdened with appointments and
their desks are stacked with papers. Finding time for an inquisitive
bore is an imposition and seldom an aspect of their official duties that
can not be postponed. But they still have to eat and a good luncheon
in congenial surroundings is often a welcome escape, not merely from
the office canteen, but from the office itself. Nowadays influence and
information are no longer the monopoly of those so rich or so well
connected as to be indifferent to hospitality. Even the really blasés
often shed at their host's table the taciturnity that grips them behind
their own desk. These phenomena are so well known – even writers
occasionally secure contracts or reviews, to say nothing of
information, across the luncheon table – that criticism of their
exploitation in diplomacy can scarcely be ascribed to rational motives.

The most productive entertainment is usually *tête à tête*, but even that most derided and, for the host, most disagreeable of diplomatic institutions, the cocktail party, has its utility. It gives real pleasue to many of the guests, particularly the useful but unsophisticated, some of whom will travel hundreds of miles to attend. It also earns the ambassador invitations to many other functions, where half an hour's attendance may enable him to extract from half-a-dozen guests information otherwise unobtainable. There are many politically delicate questions which can not readily be asked over the telephone and for which early appointments are seldom conceded, but which may be freely answered in the casual ambiance of a party by those with whom previous hospitality has created a superficial intimacy.

There can be no doubt that this is not how the world should be. In a better state of society everybody, no matter how busy or important, will gladly sacrifice all other considerations to the promotion of international amity, including the enlightenment of importunate ambassadors, at short notice and in office hours. Meanwhile much must be done, not as it should, but as it can.

Wining and dining is only part of an ambassador's functions, though it assists him in most of the rest: touring the country, visiting factories and institutions, expounding his government's policies to local audiences, having his speeches reported, meeting people, gathering their opinions. This is the general acquisition of information and dissemination of views that can not be accomplished by a visitor. Naturally a distinguished visitor will have access, even if it is arranged by the Embassy, to important people, but he will not have the constant and diffused immersion in the local culture of the resident ambassador.

These advantages are not always productive. A longer and more entertaining essay could be written on the Errors of Ambassadors. The worst – and it nowadays is all too frequent – is for the ambassador to lose his objectivity through excessive commitment to a policy he has perhaps helped to form. There are also ambassadors who have become lazy or tired; too many keep an indifferent table; a few are positively stupid and one or two of those most esteemed at home are misled by the exuberance of their own self-confidence into believing themselves exempt from those courtesies imposed by convention only on lesser men. But the failings of individuals should not be allowed to invalidate the system. The ideal ambassador, whether as defined by the traditional writers or by modern radicals, does not exist. But the average resident ambassador, with all his

frequent faults, is a rather better instrument for the understanding
and manipulation of international relations than the fleeting visitors,
the journalists or the self-styled experts with whom he is usually
contrasted. Experience has, at least, made him aware of his own
limitations.

Stripped of the trivia which command most attention, from
sociologists no less than members of the public, the idea of diplomacy
based on overseas representation is most threatened by the emergence
and growth of two rival concepts: policy-fragmentation and crisis-
management. The first assumes an international consensus in
principle and relies, for the resolution of actual disputes, on breaking
down relations with foreigners into a multitude of discrete issues to
be decided on their technical merits. This concept rejects diplomacy
because it sees no need for foreign policy. Crisis-management, on the
other hand, is much preoccupied by disputes between nation-states,
but rejects the evolutionary approach to their resolution. Diplomatic
exchanges, in this view, cut no ice. Instead disagreement must be
'signalled' by acts of violence, by ostentatious military precautions, by
economic retorsion or, in less important cases, by public insults
publicly exchanged. These create the atmosphere of crisis which alone
can engender the compromise to be negotiated, at the highest level, by
airborne special envoys. These two concepts might perhaps be
regarded, respectively, as the homoeopathic and surgical alternatives
to the conventional and conservative medicine of diplomacy.[16]

It is the patient who should make the choice, though his opinion is
unlikely to be sought or heeded. But he can still try and, before
deciding how to exert his feeble influence, he may care to consider, in
the light of the preceding arguments, a possible analogy between the
case for the resuscitation of diplomacy and Churchill's celebrated
defence of democracy: 'the worst form of government except all
those other forms that have been tried from time to time'.[17]

6 The Falklands Conflict

The causes and character of the Falklands conflict are widely misunderstood. That is scarcely surprising. So many different people had reasons of their own for complicating a straightforward issue.

Argentina wanted the Falklands Islands. Having failed, after many years of effort, to get them by negotiation, she tried coercion. On 2 April 1982 she made definitive use of limited naval force to seize these virtually undefended islands. It was a classical exertion of gunboat diplomacy to create a *fait accompli* which the victim could not resist and to which he could only respond by acquiescence or by war.

There is no reason to suppose that anyone in Argentina intended or expected war, to which gunboat diplomacy is an alternative. General Galtieri, then President, probably believed his own description of 'an English reaction' as 'scarcely possible and totally improbable'. He presumably expected protests, appeals to the United Nations, the rupture of diplomatic relations, the breaking of embassy windows and all the usual spluttering of impotent indignation. Why should the British fight for distant and rather unimportant islands they had failed to defend?

The question was – and still is – asked in other capitals than Buenos Aires.

A candid answer calls for recognition that a nation's response to foreign coercion is inevitably influenced by its international standing. The position of a Super Power is secure, both in its own eyes and in those of the world. It can afford to treat the challenges of lesser powers on their merits and to allow a cool calculation of profit or loss to determine the choice between acquiescence and war. The sheer force of statistics makes the United States a Super Power and its stature is not diminished if it yields to an isolated act of coercion by North Korea or Iran. A challenge from an equal – from the Soviet Union – would naturally be a different matter.

Nor does anyone expect a small country to stand up to greatly superior strength. If national survival is at stake, desperate resistance may be attempted and ultimately prove rewarding, but small countries

103

are not diminished by submitting to minor coercion at the hands of great powers. If small countries do fight, it is for internal reasons of their own, not to preserve an international standing they do not possess.

Medium powers are more awkwardly placed. Some aspire to greater influence and status than the statistics of their military and economic strength would altogether justify. Their standing in the world depends as much on their reputation as it does on their measurable assets. They can not afford humiliation, least of all at the hands of another country in that debatable middle ground between the Super Powers and the minor nations.

If Britain had submitted to Argentine coercion, even on an issue which affected no vital British interest, she would have lost much of her credibility either as an ally or as an enemy. And the shrillest in voicing this conclusion would have been those foreign critics who denounced Britain's actual choice as 'over-reaction'. Countries who disturb international tranquillity, even as victims, never escape censure, but there are worse fates than being classified among the wicked animals who defend themselves when attacked.

Naturally it would have been better never to have been attacked at all. This could have been avoided in two ways: by giving Argentina what she wanted in peaceful negotiations; or by convincing her that attempted coercion could only lead to the war she probably never intended.

The impediment to the first option was frankly sentimental. There was no long-term advantage to Britain in retaining the Falklands. Submarine oil and krill and the exploitation of the Antarctic were not remunerative assets in the face of constant Argentine hostility – not from bases eight thousand miles away. On any material calculus the islands were a liability. The snag was that they were inhabited.

This was an argument which cut little ice, as the Argentine delegate to the United Nations made clear in 1965: 'there is not the least doubt that the territory of the Falkland Islands is much more important than the population'. His words occasioned no surprise. In the Western hemisphere, particularly in Argentina, an indigenous people has always been an endangered species. In the wider world many decades have passed since general enthusiasm greeted President Wilson's declaration that 'peoples and provinces shall not be bartered about from sovereignty to sovereignty as if they were but chattels or pawns in the game'.[1] Since 1918 between fifty and a hundred (depending on the definition of a 'people') have been bartered in just that way. By

1982 what passes for international opinion was not interested in the wishes of the Falklanders.

In Britain the case was different, because the islanders are British. Even that massive work of propaganda, the three-volume *Historia Completa de las Malvinas*, published at Buenos Aires in 1966 by J. L. Muñoz Azpiri, admits that 'almost the entire population is of British descent'. Sixteen years of negotiation were thus devoted to a fruitless search for a compromise acceptable to both the islanders and Argentina. A hard-headed calculation of national interests might have imposed a transfer of sovereignty, coupled with the full costs of resettling, in Britain or elsewhere, those islanders reluctant to accept Argentine rule, but no British political party was willing to assume responsibility for turning British citizens out of their homes to appease a foreign power.

This was excusable. What was deplorable was British failure to draw the obvious military conclusion: the need to defend the Falkland Islands or, at the very least, to provide a convincing deterrent to attack. Ever since the end of the Second World War Argentina had demonstrated both the seriousness of her purpose and her readiness to contemplate the use of force. Britain had manifested increasing willingness to negotiate while steadily reducing the size, the capability and the relevant deployment of her armed forces, particularly her navy. That combination was asking for trouble, for just the kind of bold stroke which Argentina attempted.

Considerations of domestic politics apart, this inconsequent attitude had two underlying causes of more general application. The first was the widespread belief, by no means confined to Britain, that force had lost its potency as an instrument for the resolution of international disputes. The second was undue preoccupation with the single threat and the single scenario.

The first notion seems odd to anyone aware that significant armed conflicts have recently been averaging five a year. Nevertheless it has some rational basis. Those who help to mould public opinion, whether in Britain or in the United States, have correctly noted that force has failed the governments of both countries on a number of occasions. Britain did not get her way over the Suez Canal or Icelandic fisheries. The United States accepted defeat in Vietnam and submitted to humiliation at the hands of North Korea (the PUEBLO) and Iran (the Embassy hostages). Many other instances were invoked to support the proposition that force either had to be total (in which case it destroyed everything and everybody) or else it had to yield to the power of nationalism, ideology, politics or international opinion. In particular, it was confidently, generally and repeatedly asserted: 'the days of gunboat diplomacy are over'.

These were ethnocentric views, based on the assumption that the strong were predestined to victory. If force did not ensure success, then there was something wrong with force. Few of the critics bothered to enquire what expedients had been preferred by Egypt, North Korea, Iceland, Vietnam, Iran and the rest of the successful.

The answer, of course, was appropriate force, which is no more closely related to power than it is to morality. What is appropriate force depends on the nature of the dispute, its location, the identity and motivation of the contestants, the constraints of time and the influence of the international environment. Sometimes two policemen can do more than a carrier battle group.

Nevertheless, over that large part of the world accessible from the sea the flexibility and versatility of navies gives them exceptional opportunities to provide appropriate force – which must always, if it is to be appropriate, vary from one dispute to another. This is particularly true of islands. Five islands, groups of islands or parts of islands changed hands in the seventies through the application of force that was appropriate, limited and naval.

Iran took Greater and Lesser Tumb at the mouth of the Persian Gulf; China seized the Paracels and, first South Vietnam then the Vietnamese Liberation Navy, the Spratleys; Indonesia occupied East Timor, and Turkey a substantial slice of Cyprus. In every case protest rained impartially upon the just and the unjust. But the changes produced by gunboat diplomacy have so far endured.

Argentina, whose navy commissioned in 1977 a translation of a book called *Gunboat Diplomacy*, had every reason to expect a similar result in 1982. In Britain that popular lullaby 'the days of gunboat diplomacy are over' had closed complacent eyes to the possibility that a tool unfashionable at home might still be usable abroad.

Naturally the Royal Navy did not share these illusions about the obsolescence of force. Its exercise was their profession. But naval eyes were fixed on the Soviet Northern Fleet and such attention as could be spared from the struggle for survival against economising politicians was devoted to planning and preparation for the Third Battle of the Atlantic. This preoccupation with the single threat and the single scenario was forced on the Navy by the political necessity to justify their continued existence in terms of their contribution to NATO strategy. When coupled with financial stringency, it had the unfortunate result of eroding the flexibility, the versatility and the autonomous capability of the Royal Navy and of gradually reducing them to the auxiliary rôle of a specialised anti-submarine force.

It was sheer luck that General Galtieri struck before the process had gone too far: before the carrier INVINCIBLE had been transferred to Australia, or the assault ships FEARLESS and INTREPID had been scrapped, or the dockyard workers, who fitted out the task force with redundancy notices in their pockets, had finally disappeared. Even so, prodigies of improvisation were needed to assemble the task force, with its fleet train of requisitioned merchant ships, for its distant mission.

Sixteen years, after all, had passed since the British Ministry of Defence had proclaimed the phasing out of strike carriers and had formally renounced, as beyond future British capabilities, 'the landing, or withdrawal, of troops against sophisticated opposition outside the range of land-based air cover'.[2]

The successful achievement of the officially impossible reflects the highest credit on the Royal Navy, but very little on those decision-makers who imposed on the Navy this hazardous, costly and needless task.

In Britain the argument can still be heard that the peace-time defence of the Falklands was impracticable: it would have cost too much and tied up forces badly needed elsewhere. Life itself, to use the Russian phrase, has disposed of that contention. Not only has the recapture of the Falklands cost far more – in lives and ships and equipment, as well as money – than many years of peace-time defence, but no peace-time precautions would ever have left NATO so naked in the Narrow Seas. What is more, now that blood has been shed, it is likely that the defence of the Falklands will have to continue for years to come, perhaps not on the present scale but at a higher level than would once have been sufficient.

What was needed, years ago, was not a garrison or a naval presence capable of defeating all-out attack, but sufficient forces in place to make serious fighting impossible to avoid. This would have convinced Argentina – and mere words unsupported by visible preparations never convince anybody – that the Falklands could only be seized at the cost of war. It is most unlikely that, before 2 April 1982, she ever regarded war as an acceptable expedient.

Even lesser measures might have had a deterrent value. In June 1981 the British Ministry of Defence declared: 'We intend to resume from 1982 onwards the practice of sending a substantial naval task group on long detachment for visits and exercises in the South Atlantic [and elsewhere].' If that intention had been implemented, and implemented earlier, successive visits by separate task groups would at least have demonstrated resolution and capacity.

Deterrence is fallible and defence expensive, but both are in every way preferable to counter-attack. That final option ultimately became inevitable, but only because a succession of British governments had refused to admit the necessity of an admittedly distasteful choice: to cede the islands or to defend them.

The successful execution of that counter-attack has brought to a satisfactory conclusion the chapter that opened with the Argentine invasion of 2 April 1982, but it is by no means the end of the story. On the contrary, we are only beginning to discern the far-reaching implications for the future of these dramatic events.

In Britain, of course, there is a natural preoccupation with the present and the past. Grief at the losses incurred is mingled with pride in the conduct of the campaign, the first significant naval conflict for 37 years and one of the most remarkable operations of limited war in recent times. Indeed, it is hard to recall any precedent for an opposed landing at such a distance that achieved its objective against sophisticated opposition and superior numbers with so few casualties and in so short a time.

Naturally there will be a post-mortem. The first battle of the Falklands, in 1914, was also a popular naval victory, but it revealed serious deficiencies in British gunnery and only public acclaim saved Admiral Sturdee from professional censure. It is unlikely that, on this occasion, the successful British commanders have anything to fear, but there are obviously many lessons to be learned from the performance in combat of particular weapon systems, ships or even tactics. The Falklands War will be as important a subject of study for sailors – and not only in Britain – as the 1973 Arab–Israeli War has been for soldiers and airmen. And for the same reason. It is the latest combat test of a whole range of equipment and ideas that were previously of conjectural value. Analysis of this conflict is bound to influence the evolution of professional thinking in many armed forces, but particularly in those of Britain, because there the vocational interest will be reinforced by political engagement.

In Britain, indeed, the political repercussions are likely to be even more important than the professional. This is not just because the question earlier discussed – why did Britain ever get herself into this situation? – is due to be examined. In Britain the results of official investigations are usually bland. But popular attitudes towards defence in general, and the Navy in particular, have been altered by this evidence of success: the first undoubted and spectacular achievement for a very long time. Confrontation with Indonesia, from 1963 to 1966, produced complete success with fewer casualties, in three years, than one day's fighting in Vietnam or 74 days around the Falklands, but it lacked dramatic impact and has been largely forgotten.

These results should be of advantage to Britain's allies. Defence expenditure, particularly on the Navy, will be more acceptable. The likelihood that the next British government would insist on more drastic cuts or, always a low risk, have a neutralist complexion, has greatly diminished.

Other consequences may be less welcome. British self-confidence has been fortified. They have fought a war – admittedly a small war, a limited war, a war against an inferior enemy and a war that may not yet be over – on their own and with success. What is more, the assistance Britain received from her Allies was surreptitious when it was valuable, reluctant when it was overt, neither universal nor continuous, and seasoned with much discouraging advice. This is not a cause for complaint. The terms of the North Atlantic Alliance are quite specific: they do not apply to conflicts outside the Treaty Area and such conflicts have always tended to divide the Alliance. Britain got as much help as she could reasonably have expected, but the limits have been noted.

The British are a sensible people. They know that this was a minor and, from some points of view, an irrelevant incident. They realise the strength and hostility of the Soviet Union. They are conscious of their need for NATO. There was nothing in the Falklands experience to encourage neutralism in Britain, rather the reverse. It is within the familiar framework of Alliance and of international cooperation that a degree of enhanced self-confidence may occasionally prove disconcerting to Britain's friends.

The next act of the Falklands drama is still, only days after the surrender at Port Stanley, unpredictable. Will Argentina, for instance, be able and willing to continue the conflict, and in what form? Will third countries become involved and for good or ill?

There are, however, three distinct areas in which movement, choice and change can be expected: the defence and restoration of the Falkland Islands themselves; the complex of international relations affecting the Falklands Islands; and the rôle of the Royal Navy.

It is a safe assumption that British forces will be allotted to the defence of the Falklands Islands at least until after the next British general election – say for three years. The size, composition and activities of those forces will depend on the attitude adopted by Argentina: continued hostilities; cold war and a persisting threat; a temporary passivity in the expectation of favourable developments. There is an outside chance of a negotiated settlement, but it is highly improbable, during this period, that Argentina will convincingly renounce her claim or that the British Government will again leave the islands at her mercy. Meanwhile, the improvements to the infrastructure of the Falklands needed to make good war damage and to support a substantial military presence are likely to acquire a momentum and even a political influence of their own.

Whether British defence of the islands will be supplemented by contingents from other countries is more doubtful. Politically this would be welcome to many in Britain, but the price demanded – in terms of negotiations with Argentina, concessions regarding ultimate sovereignty and even interim administration – is likely to be more than a government flushed with success will be willing, or politically able, to pay. The compromise terms offered to avoid war are no longer available now that it has been fought and won – at some cost. Militarily, the advantages of such an arrangement would, in any case, be questionable. International forces are notoriously reluctant to engage in the serious fighting of which the Argentine Air Force has shown itself capable. They are also prone to seek instructions from their own governments in any emergency.

The probability thus remains of a substantial diversion of British forces from NATO for at least three years. It could be less substantial if the Argentine attitude, for whatever reason, is not particularly menacing. It would not have to be considered substantial in any case, if it were not for the small total size of British forces, the perpetual pressures of financial stringency and the special problems of a line of communications eight thousand miles long. As it is, the upshot will be, at best, a headache for the British Ministry of Defence and a minor, but significant, problem for NATO. In the South Atlantic the difficulties will not be insuperable.

The manageability of the problem will influence the British approach to the international environment. Almost up to the surrender at Port Stanley, certainly before the success of the San Carlos landing was apparent, doubts existed in the minds even of patriotic Britons. Suez, when a clumsy policy united both Super

Powers against Britain, is a haunting and painful memory. Since 15 June 1982 international approval still seems desirable in Britain, but no longer indispensable.

None of this alters the obvious fact that a negotiated settlement is needed in the South Atlantic and that British concessions will be necessary to achieve it. What has changed is the extent of the concessions Britain will contemplate, their timing and the degree of pressure it would be prudent for Britain's allies to apply. Military action has restored to London the advantage temporarily enjoyed by Buenos Aires: the ability to wait.

What happens internationally will also have repercussions on the future of the Royal Navy. This is still uncertain. It would be too simplistic to assume that the Falklands operation had demonstrated the value of naval flexibility and versatility and secured a reprieve for the surface fleet and the much criticised INVINCIBLE class of carrier. Many Britons, sailors and civilians alike, will take this view and press for an end to naval reductions, for more ships, better ships and new weapons and equipment. Their aspirations will collide with the entrenched doctrines of the Ministry of Defence, the financial ceilings of the Treasury and Conservative insistence on reducing government expenditure.

The altered political mood and the advantage of combat experience will give the Blue Water school fresh leverage, but much of the money thus extracted will have to be spent on replacing losses and maintaining a presence in the South Atlantic. It is hard to imagine a significant strengthening of the Navy without corresponding reductions in other aspects of Britain's defence effort. There is a case for this, but it was an argument the Navy lost in 1981, when cuts were imposed on the surface fleet in order to sustain the nuclear deterrent, the continental commitment and the air defence of the British Isles.

That debate will now be reopened. The argument ought, of course, to be decided by a thorough reappraisal of British strategy and policy in the light of the national interest. It should be assisted by a careful analysis, which will have to await fuller information, of the Falklands campaign. In practice, of course, political and even sentimental factors will exercise a disproportionate influence.

This could be of some importance to Britain's allies during the aftermath of the Falklands conflict. These allies will presumably have two general objectives. The first will be to restore stability to the South Atlantic and to promote a relationship of mutual advantage with Argentina and with Latin America as a whole. The second will be to maintain Western strength and solidarity. In principle these objectives are complementary. No Western country has anything to gain by further alienating Argentina. In practice, both tact and caution will be needed in order to avoid any fresh strain on NATO while one of its more steadfast members is entering a period of reappraisal in a mood of unwonted excitement.

7   Surprise in the Falklands

'You, my dear, are surprised', the pedantic husband told his unfaithful wife. 'I am astonished.' The words might have been General Galtieri's.

The distinction is important. The Argentine invasion of the Falklands, though not its timing, was readily predictable, the British reaction was not. This has nothing to do with the existence, dearth, appreciation, neglect or suppression of intelligence reports. Spy stories are always fascinating, though connoisseurs must regret that 'The Secret of the Falklands' has yet to be graced by the photograph of a beautiful and mysterious woman, and politicians can scarcely be blamed for indulging so popular a fantasy.

It is nevertheless supremely irrelevant. NATO, the Nuclear Deterrent, and the British Army of the Rhine were not created because anyone knew when to expect a Soviet attack. No responsible Western leader has yet argued that 37 years without such an attack constitute sufficient grounds for relaxing these precautions. Proclaimed political hostility and manifest military capability have alone justified the maintenance of the most elaborate and costly defensive system in human history.

Yet it has always been easier to argue that the Soviet Union had neither the intention nor the incentive to invade Western Europe than it has been to assert similar propositions of Argentina and the Falklands. Admittedly it is seldom safe to rely on disclaimers of territorial ambitions or of warlike purposes. Scepticism in such cases is healthy, but it becomes a dangerous complacency (as the experience of *Mein Kampf* ought to have convinced us) when it informs our attitude to specific territorial claims repeatedly advanced by people able to match their words with deeds. No 'intelligence resources' were needed to reveal that Argentina intended to recover the Falklands: it was openly proclaimed by every public and official means at Argentine disposal from 1948 onwards. Only the British attitude was ambiguous.

Consider the chronology, set out on pp.117–19.

113

These events must, of course, be seen against the larger background of the progressive liquidation of the British Empire, the reduction of the Royal Navy, the general acceptance of anti-colonialism, and the growing use of force for the resolution of certain international disputes (an annual average of five significant armed conflicts). The specific pattern is one of mounting intensity in the Argentine claim and, from 1966 onwards, of increasing British readiness to negotiate, conciliate and appease.

Unfortunately, from the Argentine point of view, this readiness did not extend to the essence of their claim: sovereignty. The British persisted in talking about the wishes of the islanders, whereas the Argentine delegate to the United Nations had made his country's attitude clear as early as 1965: 'there is not the least doubt that the territory of the Falkland Islands is much more important than the population'. What the British regarded as attempts to seek a compromise were considered by Argentina as mere delaying tactics. Blithe British proposals to 'freeze the issue of sovereignty' sounded reasonable in London, but in Buenos Aires had all the harsh resonance of a Russian 'nyet'.

Exactly when the 1966 contention that 'the force of reason' would have to be replaced by 'the argument of force' became official Argentine policy will be a nice question for future historians. It was obviously inherent in the logic of the situation: a reiterated Argentine claim the British were lastingly reluctant to concede; a strong Argentine Navy and Air Force; undefended islands; the great discrepancy in distance from the respective bases; some bellicose talk and recurrent military ascendancy in Buenos Aires.

In earlier years this seemed to have been recognised in London: until 1966 the Royal Navy attached importance to the capacity to respond promptly to minor incursions and thus to manifest British resolve. That was a watershed year. Thereafter only one Argentine challenge encountered a naval response: the still obscure episode of 1977.

With that exception British actions (always regarded by foreigners as a better clue to British intentions than mere words) offered a clear enough picture. Overseas intervention capability and standing naval deployment were both being reduced. Local defence was barely token. Provocations were ignored, appeasement attempted, and minor concessions offered; but the passage of the years brought no yielding on the essential issue of sovereignty. The British seemed to have renounced every expedient but procrastination. In Buenos Aires the argument must have seemed persuasive that the British would never move of their own accord, but that they were ready to be pushed. If Iceland could do it, in years of attrition, how much easier for Argentina to create a swift and bloodless *fait accompli*. This was a dream which became progressively more practicable and more attractive as drastic repression consolidated the power, if not the popularity, of the ruling military junta.

All that is odd about that argument is that it was evidently not perceived in London as obvious. When Argentina invaded the Falkland Islands, the Chief of the British Defence Staff was reported as saying: 'There were no contingency plans on the shelf, we had to improvise.'[1] The improvisation was brilliant but, as one of the Admiral's predecessors had earlier pointed out, counter-attack is inevitably more costly – in lives, ships, equipment and political damage, as well as money – than either defence or deterrence. Why was neither attempted?

The answers are complex and manifold, but one contention must be disposed of at the outset. Neither was ever impracticable, only inconvenient: to admirals focusing their binoculars on the Third Battle of the Atlantic, to economists slicing away at the defence estimates; to politicians sensitive to accusations of belligerence; to diplomats dreaming of an Argentina denied the substance but satisfied with the shadow of her claim. Increasingly inconvenient as the locust years went by, but impossible? – never.

Life itself, as the Russians are fond of saying, has swept that argument into the dust-bin of history. The money spent on the Falklands War, to say nothing of the reequipment, the restoration, the continued defence that will have to follow it, would have paid for years of peace-time defence or deterrence. Neither would have required a force capable of repelling any attack, merely sufficient strength to make serious fighting inevitable and pose a credible threat of war.

There is no evidence that anyone in Argentina intended or expected war – merely the definitive use of limited naval force to create a *fait accompli* that is the classical expedient of 'gunboat diplomacy'. Five other states were in undisturbed possession of islands, or parts of islands thus acquired during the 1970s,[2] and General Galtieri had every reason to consider 'an English reaction' as 'scarcely possible and totally improbable'. It would have been different if there had been a defensive force on the islands, or even that 'substantial naval task group' which the Ministry of Defence talked (but only talked) of sending 'on long detachments for visits and exercises in the South Atlantic'.

Deterrence (for the concept embraces partial defence) is naturally fallible, but it has worked so far with the Soviet Union; and there is no obvious reason why it should not have worked with Argentina. It was militarily practicable – a fraction of what was done in 1982 would have sufficed from 1966 onwards – and if it was not politically acceptable (because it presupposed the possibility, in the event of failure, of fighting for the Falklands), the logical consequence should have been admitted and the Falklands ceded to Argentina. Tough luck on the islanders? But they would have been only one of a hundred peoples, since 1918, to suffer the world's denial of President Woodrow Wilson's ringing declaration that 'peoples and provinces shall not be bartered about from sovereignty to sovereignty as if they were but chattels or pawns in the game'. They could have been compensated by the United Kingdom citizenship that the present government has denied them, and by the full costs of their resettlement in the country of their choice. It is for professed moralists to decide whether such a solution would have been more or less iniquitous than a war of uncertain final outcome; but the ordinary man may regard it as more decent than retaining the allegiance of the islanders while denying them protection.

This statement of the dilemma provides the first answer to the complex of questions stemming from Argentine success in surprising the British on 2 April 1982. No British government, no British parliament, no British political party – at least since 1966 – had been willing to face the crucial choice: cede the Falkland Islands or defend them. Nor had their professional advisers been determined to press this choice upon them.

The promised official enquiry will doubtless produce many rationalisations of this indecision. There may even be embarrassing 'revelations', when particular documents seem to crystallise, at this or that moment, the prevailing mood of unjustified complacency. These are likely to be quite beside the point. When Admiral Ciliax humiliated the British Government, successfully taking the SCHARNHORST and the GNEISENAU from Brest up the Channel back to Germany in 1942, many more or less plausible excuses were forthcoming for the failure to predict the date of the operation or even to detect the squadron's sailing. What mattered was that the long-expected move would have succeeded whenever it was attempted, because no adequate preparations had been made to counter it. In the case of the Falklands, there is little reason to disbelieve General Galtieri's statement to Miss Oriana Fallaci that: 'if the military events had not taken place on the second of April 1982, the same thing would have happened in April or May or June next year, or one of the following years' (*The Times*, 12 June 1982). A standing threat can only be deterred by standing – and visible – precautions.

What the enquiry may help to identify is the moment by which this view, already suggesting itself in 1966, should have become irresistible in London. If a particular year is thus selected, the choice may well seem unfair to those it spotlights. And so it probably will be. If the slowly mounting wave of Argentine irredentism surprised the British when it finally overwhelmed the Falklands, the cause should not be sought in the particular errors of individuals, but in the deficiencies of the conventional wisdom. Alas, force is not obsolete, nor are the days of gunboat diplomacy over. The necessity for choice is not to be evaded by procrastination. Foreigners do exist and, even when Latin American, must sometimes be taken seriously. There is more than one threat and the single scenario is a delusion as certifiable as conveniently early warning time. It is still as true today as it was when the Foreign Office said (in 1907) that: 'The opportune presence of a British ship of war may avert a disaster which can only be remedied later at much inconvenience and considerable sacrifice.'

Year	Argentine manifestation	British response	International
1948	Special department founded in Foreign Ministry to press claim		Britain yields to force and withdraws from Palestine
	Navy demonstrates in Antarctic	HMS NIGERIA sent to scene	
1950	Senate and Chamber of Deputies declare Falklands to be Argentine territory		
1953	Attempted naval occupation of Deception Island	HMS SNIPE sent to expel intruders	
1955	Argentina rejects jurisdiction of International Court of Justice or of 'any other judicial or arbitral tribunal'		
1960			UN General Assembly pass

Year	Argentine manifestation	British response	International
			Resolution no. 1514 calling for an end to colonialism
1963			Britain withdraws from Kenya
1965			General Assembly call for negotiations on Argentine claim to Falklands
1966	Military *coup d'état* Navy shell a Soviet trawler	Foreign Secretary visits Buenos Aires for talks on claim	
	'Condor Commandos' invade the Falklands in a hijacked airliner	HMS PUMA sent to Falklands	
	'The Argentine people must realise that one day they will have to employ the argument of force' (*Historia Completa de las Malvinas*)	Ministry of Defence renounces carriers and 'landing . . . of troops against sophisticated opposition outside the range of land-based air cover'	
1968		Chalfont mission to Buenos Aires and Falklands	
1970	Military *coup d'état*	Naval presence reduced to visits by ice-patrol ship	
1971	Anglo-Argentine Agreement on communications with Falklands via Argentina		British inaction in face of Iran's seizure of islands in Persian Gulf
1974	Press and opposition politicians demand invasion of Falklands		British inaction in face of Turkish invasion of Cyprus
1975	Attempted military coup		
1976	Military *coup d'état* Occupation of South Thule	Silence	Britain finally concedes her defeat by Iceland
	Argentina initiates withdrawal of Ambassadors in protest against Shackleton visit Navy fires on British ship	Shackleton visits Falklands	

Year	Argentine manifestation	British response	International
1977	Anglo-Argentine talks are resumed. Navy commissions translation of *Gunboat Diplomacy*		Britain backs Chile against Argentina over Beagle Channel dispute
	Navy use force to capture six Soviet trawlers and factory ship on high seas		
	Invasion scare	HM Ships DREADNOUGHT, PHOEBE, ALACRITY and two auxiliaries sent to South Atlantic	
1978	Successful Argentine naval demonstration against Chile		
	Anglo-Argentine talks on Falklands adjourned		
1979	Ambassadors return to their posts		
1980		Ridley fails to persuade Falkland Islanders of the need for concessions to Argentina	Iran imposes her will on the USA UN General Assembly support independence for Belise in spite of Guatemalan claim

Hence no progress in Anglo-Argentine talks.

8   Surprise and the Single Scenario

Surprise being the theme and the Falklands the scene of the latest example, it is worth recalling how those islands were invaded. After the British had dismissed protests and ignored previous incidents, five frigates with 1600 soldiers aboard left Buenos Aires undetected and, out of the blue, arrived off the islands and delivered an ultimatum. This was rejected and the invading troops landed under cover of a bombardment by the frigates. The British marines ashore[1] – two officers and 21 other ranks – fired a few shots for honour's sake, then, seeing the impossibility of defence against such a force, capitulated.

In London there was intense indignation, not only at the invasion, but at the Government's failure to foresee and prevent it. The Foreign Secretary had to resign and, without waiting for a reply to diplomatic protests, a powerful task force was quickly fitted out at Portsmouth. The Foreign Secretary's name, by the way, was Lord Weymouth, for that invasion took place in 1770.

Those who will not learn from history are doomed to repeat it, but that is not the point of the story. It is the merest prelude to a question. How does surprise happen?

STRATEGIC SURPRISE

Strategic surprise, that is. Tactical surprise is commonplace, something every commander strives for in any kind of war. He attacks the waiting enemy earlier than expected, from an unforeseen direction, in a strength, using weapons or with a speed never predicted. Strategic surprise is the fate of the enemy who is not awaiting any attack at all. Perhaps he does not even know he is an enemy, or else he thinks that his own strength or his alliances or distance or natural obstacles have given him immunity. He may

120

believe in the sovereign virtues of a non-aggression pact, of neutrality, of international law. He may rely on the protection of the United Nations. He may even have concluded that there was no point in attempting a defence which could only be futile. The last kind of enemy, however, is a sitting bird and attacking him should not be dignified as strategic surprise.

Strategic surprise usually begins a war, as it did when the Japanese attacked Port Arthur in 1904 or Pearl Harbor in 1941; when Hitler invaded Russia in 1941 or the Arabs launched an offensive against Israel in 1973. So it did in April 1982, when Argentina seized the Falklands, even though General Galtieri neither intended nor expected his action to start a war. 'An English reaction was,' he thought, 'scarcely possible and totally improbable.'[2] Strategic surprise is also occasionally possible even after war has begun. The German invasion of Norway in 1940 is a case in point. The Norwegians were surprised because they believed themselves protected by their neutrality. The British were so convinced that their naval superiority made invasion impossible that even last-minute intelligence of German movements did not persuade the Admiralty to deploy the fleet accordingly. It was their failure that earned the luckless Commander-in-Chief the nickname of 'Wrong Way Charlie'. And, of course, British eyes were fixed on the Central – sorry – Western Front.

For the victim strategic surprise is usually a self-inflicted wound. It is his complacency which provides the essential condition for successful surprise. He knows – he cannot help knowing – the hostility and the capability of the adversary. But, the victim tells himself: they would never dare. Sometimes they do.

Two centuries ago the Earl of Chatham, who had some experience of high policy, laid the blame for Spanish aggression against the Falklands squarely on the British Government. 'Before the country they stand', he said, 'as the greatest criminals. They have done everything that they ought not to have done, and hardly anything that they ought to have done.'[3]

Some of the lessons of strategic surprise have since been learned. The fear of surprise attack has prompted the most elaborate, the most frightening precautions ever known in the history of the human race. In North America, in Europe, in the Soviet Union, in China, in a large part of the world's oceans, there are ballistic nuclear missiles with a readiness sometimes measured in fewer minutes than their flight time. The pins are out of the grenades and we can only hope that no cramp develops in the tense fingers clutching their levers.

MODERN SURVEILLANCE

Readiness for retaliation is matched by the vast apparatus of modern surveillance: radar chains, satellites, electronic eavesdropping, clandestine reconnaissance, even espionage on a scale never previously attempted. The volume, detail and accuracy of the information now available to members of the public concerning the order of battle of the world's principal military powers exceeds the wildest dreams of any intelligence service in 1939. And only submarines can hope that their movements will be unobserved. It might almost be thought that strategic surprise was now technically impossible.

For several reasons this is not the case. Surveillance may have attained a precision hitherto undreamt of, but the significant changes, the indicators, it is required to detect have become almost microscopic. Today the main forces of the principal military powers are not only in place, but in presence. It is no longer possible for staff officers to comfort themselves with the thought that the enemy's mobilisátion will at once be detected, that the process can scarcely begin before the harvest has been completed and that it will then take a defined number of days, even weeks. Nuclear war needs no mobilisation.

Conventional war on land could not, admittedly, erupt quite so quickly, but acceleration from a standing start could nevertheless be much faster than ever before, faster, perhaps, than is usually accepted. The Belgian General Robert Close made himself very unpopular in NATO circles by his scenario for a Soviet surprise attack that reached the Rhine in 48 hours. Admittedly his calculations made little allowance for those mishaps and blunders to which the Red Army are surely quite as prone as any other, but, to a layman, his general line of argument was uncomfortably plausible.[4]

Little need be said about air forces, whose peace-time readiness is now often of Battle of Britain standards, to say nothing of standing air patrols and airborne nuclear bombers. Their capacity for strategic surprise was demonstrated by the Israelis in 1967.

Navies, perhaps, might be regarded as the principal victims of modern technology. Their traditional ability to make an unexpected appearance from a clouded horizon has suffered greatly from the installation of infrared sensors in satellites. Even navies, however, now enjoy some compensating advantages. The student of naval history, for instance, soon becomes familiar with the many hours at which warships used to be at notice 'for steam' and with the paralysing importance of fuel consumption. Sail too late and you missed the enemy; sail too soon and you ran out of fuel, as did all but two of the many British warships that hunted the BISMARCK in 1941. Nowadays gas turbines can be 'flashed up' in minutes and tankers accompany the fleet and refuel ships at sea. A fleet can now deploy early, pose a threat and then wait for the right moment.

Even a commander as dilatory as Admiral Sturdee need no longer be caught, if not with his trousers down, at least in his pyjamas, at the first battle of the Falklands in 1914. His ships were coaling when the enemy arrived. Greater German boldness might have crushed them in Port Stanley harbour. Fortunately von Spee missed his chance and neither Sturdee's faulty tactics nor the deficiencies of British gunnery could prevent the destruction of the German squadron by a superior force. Nor, as it happened, did the handicaps suffered by modern navies prevent Argentina from achieving complete strategic surprise at Port Stanley on 2 April 1982.

POLITICAL JUDGMENT

The military conditions for surprise have undergone many changes in the last 50 years. It is not easy to strike an appropriate balance among the conflicting factors of improved surveillance, greater peace-time readiness, enhanced acceleration from a standing start and faster reaction times. A reasonable conclusion might be that everything would happen much more quickly if it happened at all. But it is not clear, in relation to this increased tempo, that military indicators alone necessarily provide earlier or more reliable evidence of enemy intentions than they did at any previous period. It is unfortunately still necessary to rely on an intangible, subjective, inherently undependable factor: political judgment. Do the ambiguous, but observable, actions of the adversary reveal an intention so probable as to demand precautions?

One reason for this unfortunate state of affairs is that threatening behaviour has become normal in our era of violent peace. In 1893 we almost went to war with France because a French cruiser had turned her guns on a British cruiser. This was then the ultimate naval insult, an extreme provocation. The Kaiser, then visiting Queen Victoria at Cowes, was shown the telegrams and expressed the opinion, with evident satisfaction, that there was no way out but war. In 1973 it was all in the day's work for groups of Soviet warships to make dummy attacks on the carriers of the Sixth Fleet. The warships, particularly the submarines, of the principal powers, together with their military aircraft, are constantly probing each other's defences. Even neutral Sweden has been averaging ten visits a year from 'unidentified' submarines. As for armies, Check Point Charlie was the scene of some notable confrontations. Intelligence experts strive to establish definite criteria for discriminating between manoeuvres, probes and warning signals, on the one hand, and the approach march to contact, on the other, but their task is not easy. Least of all if they happen, as sometimes occurs, to be looking in the wrong direction.

The exercise of political judgment is even more difficult. This has to be attempted on the basis of much less hard intelligence than is available in the military field. The intentions of the adversary – the most critical factor – can only be guessed: they can never be known. During the closing stages of the 1973 War, for instance, the two Super Powers exchanged menacing messages about intervention in the Middle East and reinforced these diplomatic communications by ostentatious military precautions and a naval confrontation in the Mediterranean. Did either government seriously contemplate war with the other? It is doubtful whether either President Brezhnev or President Nixon was sure of his own intentions.

Similarly, in 1969, the Russians deliberately leaked the story that they were contemplating a pre-emptive nuclear strike against China. Was this a bluff intended to put pressure on the Chinese over the border conflict then active? Was it a probe to discover what American reactions might be? Or was someone in Moscow sabotaging a serious plan by premature disclosure? I do not see how anyone outside the Kremlin – or most of those within its walls – could ever expect to know. In the case of the Soviet Union, of course, this uncertainty is aggravated by the traditional – and very effective – Russian secrecy, but the intentions of other governments are often equally obscure. How soon, I wonder, did the commander of the Falklands Task Force know for certain that his voyage was meant to end in action?

WARNING TIME

Against this background of inevitable uncertainty it is curious, even paradoxical, that NATO strategy should place such reliance on the concept of 'political warning time'.

Publicly, of course, the Ministry of Defence are commendably cautious. 'NATO would therefore expect to receive some warning of Soviet preparation for war, though the amount of warning time would vary depending on the balance the Soviet leaders chose between surprise and preparedness.'⁵ In actual fact NATO strategy makes no kind of sense unless warning time is measured in many weeks. 'The conventional defence of Central Europe', according to the Ministry, 'depends crucially on transatlantic reinforcement and resupply – the bulk of equipment and resupply would have to come by sea.'⁶ Field Marshal Lord Carver has also told us:

> Unless those reinforcements and supplies reach this side of the Atlantic before hostilities start – then I have not much hope, whether they come by air or by sea, that they will be very relevant to the situation.⁷

On this basis my own very rough estimate of the warning time needed is eight weeks. This has three main components. The first and least predictable is indecision time: the period during which Allied governments debate the significance of the ambiguous signals reaching them from the East; argue whether mobilisation would be prudent or provocative; and delay for the doubters, so as to avoid giving an impression of disunity. The second is loading time: the period needed to assemble men, equipment and supplies; to gather and load shipping; to divert American warships from the Pacific and the Indian Ocean. The third is transit time: the organisation of convoys, their passage across the Atlantic, unloading at this end and movement to the operational area.

This estimate may seem unduly pessimistic in the light of the Falklands experience, but that had special features which would have no place in the kind of crisis we have been considering. The starting signal was unmistakable: invasion of the islands. Only one government had to take a decision. The absence of time pressure and, for most of the voyage out, of opposition meant that the Task Force could be built up piecemeal and en route. Most important of all: the despatch of the Task Force did not in itself expose Britain to any kind of danger from Argentina. Compared to sending reinforcements to the Central Front, which might actually precipitate a Soviet attack, this was an easy decision and could be taken promptly.

It was, of course, also an indication of British reliance on warning time, that the Government did not hesitate to strip NATO of most of its naval defence in the eastern Atlantic for many weeks and to reduce to derisory proportions and for a similar period British ability to provide reinforcements for the Central Front, for Norway, for the Atlantic islands or for anywhere else in the NATO area.

Nor is Britain alone in adopting this attitude. The United States have for years been cutting their Second Fleet, in the Atlantic, to the bone in order to provide forces in the Indian Ocean or other distant seas. Even the Sixth Fleet, in the Mediterranean, has been reduced to a single carrier, even though the Supreme Allied Commander Atlantic says he would need four carrier battle groups for war in either the Mediterranean or the Norwegian Sea. And, if the Rapid Deployment Force ever becomes involved in the Persian Gulf, or the Middle East, or Latin America, or Taiwan or Korea, the availability of air and ground reinforcements for the Central Front will be much reduced.

NOT THE CENTRAL FRONT

Strategic surprise, it seems to me, is still possible, but I do not think it will happen on the Central Front. On that front the concept of political warning time has considerable plausibility. Not because of any technical or military obstacles to surprise attack but because the risks of escalation would so greatly exceed any foreseeable advantages. It is difficult to devise any scenario for a Soviet assault on the Central Front that does not carry a high risk of nuclear war. Nor is it easy to imagine what advantages even the most optimistic of Soviet leaders, someone who expected conventional victory to lead to negotiation, even capitulation, rather than escalation, would hope to gain by running such appalling risks. Eastern Europe is enough of a headache without adding a sullen, resentful, partially destroyed slice of Western Europe to the Kremlin's problems. Such a decision is not only inherently improbable, but it would be contested, reluctant, slow to emerge. Soviet governments have always been less adventurous than American. Stalin's dithering in 1941, in the face of the mounting evidence of Hitler's planned aggression, was enough to make Neville Chamberlain appear a man of instant and ruthless decision. And the contrast between Czechoslovakia in 1968 and Poland from 1980 onwards suggests that even enterprises of lower risk now require years rather than months for their resolution.

Of course, we cannot exclude the possibility of a radical change of style in the Kremlin. The arrival of new leaders, inevitable in the next few years because of the advanced age of the present Politburo, might eventually lead to the rule of a new generation, who had known the

Soviet Union only as a Super Power and who lacked the caution ingrained into their predecessors by decades of weakness and disaster. Nevertheless, in a society so dominated by experienced old men, so intent on continuity and stability, the newcomers would have to struggle to impose their power and policies. The process would surely be both gradual and visible. The rise in international tension would be progressive and preceded by turbulence within the leadership. This might well prompt the general conclusion that 'adventurism' – a boo-word in Moscow since Khrushchev's fall – was once more in fashion. NATO would then be wise to be on their guard. They might nevertheless also be foolish if they decided that even new and rasher Soviet leaders would choose, from the wealth of options open to them, so dangerous an adventure as the Central Front.

Without the existence of NATO forces on this front, of course, the risk for the Soviet Union would be much less, the prospective advantages greater and the whole equation different. Whatever Soviet intentions may be, the Group of Soviet Armies in Germany is a fact. But we should not allow the assessment of capabilities, important though this is, to exclude the consideration of probabilities. Nor should the magnitude of the gravest danger divert all attention from lesser but more likely threats.

This happened over the Falklands, most obviously in the progressive reduction of the Navy to an anti-submarine force for that improbable single scenario: the defence of seaborne reinforcement and resupply for the Central Front against Soviet naval attack. Of course, General Galtieri was foolish not to wait for the process to be completed: for INVINCIBLE to reach Australia and for HERMES, FEARLESS, INTREPID and a few more beside to arrive at the breakers. But enough had been done, down to the announced withdrawal of that token ship, ENDURANCE, to convince him that Britain had no intention of defending the islands.

Part of the trouble was that successive Chiefs of Staff, anxious to protect the Armed Forces against cuts, had over-sold the vulnerability of the Central Front. Intending to persuade the politicians that units could not safely be withdrawn from Germany, they had ended by creating the idea that maintenance of the Central Front was the one and only justification for any armed forces at all. Hence that truly extraordinary description of the United Kingdom as 'a forward base for operations in the Channel and North Sea and a rear base for operations on the Continent'.[8]

If that is how the Ministry of Defence regard the British Isles, it is scarcely surprising that they never considered providing Port Stanley with the battalion, the few Rapiers and the coastal artillery that would have been enough – not to give the islands an assured defence – but to convince Argentina that we meant business. The Ministry did, admittedly, talk – but only talk – 'of sending a substantial naval task group on long detachment for visits and exercises in the South Atlantic'.[9] Perhaps this was one of the passages in *The Way Forward* which decided General Galtieri to strike when he did, before the open window of opportunity could be closed by a British naval presence in the South Atlantic.

It may seem that I have achieved the impossible: being unfair to the Ministry of Defence. Of course, political judgment was most at fault. If Ministers had insisted that there must be a visible deterrent – a tripwire – to Argentine seizure of the Falklands, one would have been provided. This failure has nothing whatever to do with the absence, neglect or suppression, if such was the case, of intelligence about Argentine plans. One British Corps is not in Germany because anyone ever knew when to expect a Soviet attack. We see Soviet capability and we do not believe Soviet assertions that they have no territorial ambitions in Western Europe. We saw Argentine capability and we did not believe their repeated and public declarations that they intended to repossess the Malvinas. What in Europe was a healthy scepticism became, in the South Atlantic, the ostrich posture. We were kicked where we deserved to be.

Why did we invite our fate? In various articles[10] I have suggested several reasons, but here I am emphasising only one: obsession with the single scenario, with the gravest threat, whether or not this was the most likely, whether or not this was the one which Britain could most effectively counter. I do so not because I think it was necessarily the predominant reason why we were surprised on 2 April 1982 – we still have much to learn about the background – but because this factor has important lessons for the future. These are not concerned with our remaining imperial death duties – though I have thought it appropriate to say a few words elsewhere about Gibraltar[11] – but with our own, vital, insular survival. There is no law of strategy or of politics that says this survival can only be threatened by the arrival of SS20 missiles or by the advance of Soviet armour across the North Germany Plain.

LIMITED WAR

Without going into details or attempting alternative scenarios, it may be appropriate to suggest two broad principles and to draw from them an equally broad conclusion. The first principle is that the existence of a balance of nuclear terror has made total war and global war less likely, but has provided a kind of greenhouse in which lesser conflicts, now averaging five a year, can flourish. What makes limited wars and local wars frequent now and probable in the future is that such wars can be won. They can be won because even a defeat, if it is limited and local – the American defeat in Indo-China, for instance – often seems preferable to the alternative of escalation to the total war which everybody would lose. This is, of course, a preference which only the Super Powers can exercise and which may not always be shared by the belligerents themselves. They go to war – or one of them does – because they expect to win, but they do not necessarily regard their war as limited or the consequences of defeat as more tolerable than those of escalation. Such sentiments were probably foreign to both Arabs and Israelis in 1967 and again in 1973, but the decision was taken above their heads. Both Super Powers have manifested – unlike Kaiser Wilhelm II in 1914 – a high degree of tolerance for the pain and humiliation suffered by their allies. Even their own afflictions, the Soviet Union over Cuba in 1962 no less than the United States in Vietnam, are supported with greater patience than was usual in previous eras. The fear of nuclear war is the beginning of wisdom, but this wisdom is so far imperfect; it has little influence on those without the responsibility for nuclear decisions, while even governments with that responsibility believe that less momentous choices are still open to them.

Limited wars are thus likely. So far the most conspicuous, but not the only, examples have occurred outside the NATO area, but it would be wishful thinking to regard this historical accident as somehow determined by immutable principles of policy or strategy. It is not geography, nor treaties, that will decide the choice between acquiescence and escalation, but the complex and largely unpredictable equation of perceived interest and immediate fear.

The second principle is that the primary preoccupation of the Soviet Union – not Britain's only enemy, but certainly the most dangerous – is one inherited from the Tsars: their own defensive perimeter. The historical justification for this attitude is unimpeachable. The political arguments are at least understandable: it is no more than a reversal of the *cordon sanitaire* sought by Western Europe between the two wars against the menace of Bolshevism. The strategic rationale is obvious: every fortress needs a glacis and the Soviet Union lacks the convenient shield which the Atlantic and Pacific Oceans provide for the United States.

Since 1917 the Soviet Union have been mainly concerned to secure that glacis. To begin with, in their early period of weakness, they lost ground on all their western frontiers. For a long time their only gains were at the expense of China, then even weaker. Before, and at the outset of, the Second World War, when their natural enemies were divided, they regained some of their losses: in Finland, in the Baltic States, in Poland. After the Second World War, when their strength and the disunity of their enemies reached a zenith, they made important gains round the entire perimeter. Where they could not annex territory, they established satellites, zones of influence or, at the very least, of acceptable, even benevolent neutrality.

But they also had many failures: Finland (all but the eastern provinces); Austria; Berlin; Iran; Turkey; Manchuria; Albania; Yugoslavia; ultimately China. They had probed – repeatedly and over many years in the case of Berlin – but they had withdrawn when they encountered real resistance. Their policy was patient, persistent, unscrupulous, but cautious. Much more cautious than that of the United States. Above all Soviet policy was opportunist. When the circumstances – what they like to call 'the correlation of forces' – favoured them, they attempted the consolidation and even the extension of their defensive perimeter. And, of course, they pursued the contest for global influence natural to a Super Power. In neither case, however, were they inclined to rashness. Only over Cuba, in 1962, did the Soviet Union run open-ended risks. And the fact that this led to the downfall of Khrushchev has not been forgotten by his successors.

Viewed from Moscow the Soviet perimeter has obvious weaknesses and is even exposed to local irritants. The proximity to the main Soviet naval base of Norwegian airfields and the Norwegian radar chain is unwelcome. It would be more convenient if the passage of the Northern Fleet to the Norwegian Sea, already constricted by ice to starboard, had a friendly coast to port. Further south Bornholm is obnoxious for its surveillance and as the nearest hostile territory to restless Poland. The exits from the Baltic could be in safer hands, for even Sweden is not as neutral as she should be. Berlin is a cancer that has so far proved inoperable. Yugoslavia poses no military threat, but is a political menace. Albania once provided a useful submarine base and might do so again. Greece would be better out of NATO and the international régime of the Turkish Straits is no more acceptable to the Politburo than it was to the Tsars. Iran is disturbingly adjacent to the Moslem peoples of Soviet Asia, but experience in Afghanistan may have suggested that a cure could be worse than the disease. The Chinese frontier is a constant source of trouble and anxiety, as well as inconveniently close to the Trans-Siberian railway. But it is hard to believe that anyone in Moscow worries unduly about the Central Front, the thickest and most solidly defended sector of the entire perimeter.

Nothing in the Soviet record suggests that high risks would be run to remedy these imperfections, as opposed to defending and consolidating the existing perimeter. But, if the disunity of their enemies, local disturbances or Western distraction in distant adventures ever seem to offer low-cost opportunities, these are the points at which the Soviet Union might attempt political pressure, subversion, coercive diplomacy or even limited war. It may never happen, but it does seem more likely than armoured masses assaulting the Central Front. In the Northern Sector relatively small Soviet gains could create larger dangers for Britain, not least if they led to the unravelling of the Alliance. They could also be, though they are not at present, easier to counter.

THE NEED FOR FLEXIBLE RESPONSE

From these two principles there may be drawn the broad conclusion that, for Britain, flexible response is more important than forward defence. She cannot, unfortunately, afford both. To provide a better air defence of the British Isles and the surrounding seas, to maintain the naval forces needed for possible confrontations at sea, to create an amphibious intervention capability, British forces in Germany will have to be reduced. Their presence is due to an accident of history and has now become an anachronism. If the Alliance still wants forward defence on the present scale against an unlikely threat, there are other and richer allies to provide it. The British contribution should be the protection of seaborne communications and an amphibious capability that could reassure the Northern Allies in peace and reinforce them in war. Whatever she attempts, Britain can only lose a total war. But some limited wars, even in the NATO area, could be won by a maritime strategy. Such a strategy would also provide Britain with a measure of insurance against the failure of Alliance, whether through growing disunity and disaffection or as a result of a limited defeat. At present too many of Britain's eggs are in a German basket. France has been more sensible.

French policy has had the supreme merit of preserving for France a wider range of options than Britain now enjoys. Her nuclear deterrent is truly independent, the bulk of her forces are on her own soil and all of them are under her own, unfettered control. France's territory is free from foreign installations or foreign weapons. She is as near as any country can be nowadays to retaining a sovereign choice between war and peace. That choice may prove important, for even the Soviet Union is unlikely to make the mistake of attacking all its enemies at once or in a manner to which only one response is conceivable. Sudden, but ambiguous pressure on a single ally might be a fruitful form of strategic surprise, particularly if most of the opposing forces are on the Central Front and can be tied to it by demonstrative manoeuvres in East Germany.

Such arguments will naturally encounter objections from those regarding – as does John Terraine in his eloquent defence of British generalship in the First World War – the supreme objective as being 'victories won against the main body of the main enemy in a continental war'.[12] There are two flaws in this view. Such victories may not be possible for anyone in future. Even if they are, it should nevertheless be the purpose of any sensible national strategy to ensure that 'the main body of the main enemy' is fought by somebody else. John Terraine gives the game away when he extols the British victories of the First World War as 'the only time in British history'[13] when this prudent principle has been abandoned. Although it would be wrong to date Britain's decline only from the First World War, it is undeniable that it accelerated the descent of Great Britain as much as it speeded the rise of the United States, whose own policy was then as well judged as it was in the true British tradition.

The single scenario and the gravest threat are bets which Britain, surprise or no surprise, can only lose. British resources would be better spread across the spectrum of limited, likely and winnable conflicts.

9 Cant in Foreign Policy

> My dear friend, clear your mind of cant . . . you may talk in
> this manner; it is a mode of talking in society; but don't think
> foolishly.
>
> Johnson[1]

Cant has so long and so variously diversified the texture of international relations that any brief examination must necessarily
concentrate on a single aspect of this complex and controversial
phenomenon. We shall not, for instance, here be concerned with cant
as an esoteric language intended to confuse the vulgar while conveying
a specific meaning to initiates, an important function in the nineteenth
century, when an 'unfriendly act' was a phrase more precisely and
convincingly minatory than such later formulations as 'we are filled
with determination to use force to crush the aggressors'.[2] The progressive inflation of diplomatic language and its increasing divorce from
consequential action have nowadays destroyed this once useful
application of cant.

Nor is it necessary to consider, intriguing though such a study might
be, the stylistic mannerisms of particular governments. The British,
for instance, delight in such phrases as 'British public opinion attaches
great importance to the due execution of the Article in question',[3]
whereas the Russians, in a manner reminiscent of Macaulay's 'every
schoolboy knows who imprisoned Montezuma and who strangled
Atahualpa',[4] prefer 'in no other way is it possible to explain the
unalterable fact'.[5] The demonstrable untruth of such assertions – one
could spend an entire day interrogating pedestrians in Piccadilly
without discovering a single British subject who had even heard of
Article 14(d) of the Agreement on the Cessation of Hostilities in
Vietnam – is not deliberate, or systematic or consequential: it is the
merest literary aberration, an uncontrolled impetuosity of expression.

Deliberate deception, however, is not a necessary or even a distinguishing characteristic of cant. Those addicted to this mode of expression or cast of thought may believe their own words; they may be

using conventionally acceptable language to clothe controversial ideas; or they may be trying to disguise their meaning. What counts is not the sincerity of the speaker but the relationship between the impression naturally created by his words and their obvious practical implications. In the language of cant there is usually a marked discrepancy between the satisfaction, approval, toleration or indifference to be expected from those who accept the words used at their face value and the sentiments aroused in those who believe they have comprehended the full intentions, implications or assumptions of an apparently innocuous phraseology. It is the extent of this discrepancy, rather than the degree of correspondence with objective truth, that distinguishes cant from tact. When a diplomatist declines an invitation because of a prior engagement, he may be telling a flat lie, but he is giving tactful expression to a concrete and unambiguous intention: not to accept. When the United States Stategic Air Command proclaim 'peace is our profession', they are indulging in cant, even if elaborate and sophisticated arguments might be adduced to support their assertion. The discrepancy between the natural meaning of 'peace' and the real prospect of thermo-nuclear megadeaths is excessive.

Cant, therefore, will be considered here as a mode of expression, or a cast of thought, of which the effect – irrespective of the motive – is to create a misleading discrepancy between the natural meaning of words and their practical significance, a discrepancy even more dangerous when, as often happens, the speaker is as much misled as his audience.

This is a subjective and question-begging definition, but cant resembles sin: it is deplorable; it is widespread and it is committed exclusively by other people. It would thus be misleading – indeed, it might even be regarded as cant – to claim a high degree of objectivity or general acceptance for the attempt that follows to isolate from actual examples the specific characteristics of this phenomenon. Any description or definition necessarily implies certain prior assumptions of a political or quasi-philosophical character. Any conclusions reached may thus prove repugnant to those who reject their premises. These are those of realism and relativity: that, in the world as it exists, the language of governments has to be assessed by the degree of its approximation to their actions and that these actions have to be judged by their results.

This is an approach which extends the customary frontiers of cant beyond the utterances of foreign governments or even of those native statesmen of whom the reader happens to disapprove. Indeed, it is fundamental to the present argument that cant is a universal phenomenon confined to no one nation, class of men or set of ideas. It is to be found on both sides of most disputes and there have been many diplomatic exchanges, even between nation-states of similar traditions and social structures, in which each could sincerely contrast their own candour with the other's cant.

A classical example is the report by the British Ambassador in Berlin of his final interview with the German Chancellor on 4 August 1914:

> I found the Chancellor very agitated. His Excellency at once began a harangue, which lasted for about twenty minutes. He said that the step taken by His Majesty's Government was terrible to a degree; just for a word – 'neutrality', a word which in war had so often been disregarded – just for a scrap of paper Great Britain was going to make war on a kindred nation who desired nothing better than to be friends with her. All his efforts in that direction had been rendered useless by this last terrible step, and the policy to which, as I knew, he had devoted himself since his accession to office had tumbled down like a house of cards. What we had done was unthinkable; it was like striking a man from behind while he was fighting for his life against two assailants. He held Great Britain responsible for all the terrible events that might happen. I protested strongly against that statement, and said that, in the same way as he and Herr von Jagow wished me to understand that for strategical reasons it was a matter of life and death to Germany to advance through Belgium and violate the latter's neutrality, so I would wish him to understand that it was, so to speak, a matter of 'life and death' for the honour of Great Britain that she should keep her solemn engagement to do her utmost to defend belgium's neutrality if attacked. That solemn compact simply had to be kept, or what confidence could anyone have in engagements given by Great Britain in the future? The Chancellor said, 'But at what price will that compact have been kept. Has the British Government thought of that?'[6]

There is no reason to doubt Bethman-Hollweg's sincerity (Harold Nicolson, who knew him personally, described him as sharing with Sir Edward Grey 'the honour of being, alone of pre-war statesmen, morally unassailable'),[7] but few British readers have failed to detect the discrepancy between his professions of friendship and the underlying assumptions and implications so obviously revealed by the policy of his government. Yet, when one ponders on Bethman-Hollweg's final question, when one recalls Hardinge's famous minute on the British guarantee to Belgium,[8] when one studies the various interpretations accorded by British governments – before or after 1914 – to the 'honour of Great Britain', can one acquit Sir E. Goschen of an equal indulgence in cant?

Each of the participants in this dramatic dialogue was surely employing language that was only metaphorically related to the practical problems at issue. The neutrality of Belgium had not yet been threatened when the French Ambassador in London, relying on the secret staff talks concealed by Sir Edward Grey from Parliament (and for long even from his colleagues) exclaimed on 1 August: 'j'attends de savoir si le mot honneur doit être rayé du vocabulaire anglais'.[9] Nor was it his opinion alone that the honour of England was at stake before Belgium was invaded: the Permanent Under-Secretary of the Foreign Office (by this time the less cynical Sir Arthur Nicolson) had already protested to Sir Edward Grey: 'you will render us a by-word among nations'.[10] As for Bethman-Hollweg, he had been warned seriously enough to send a frantic, if futile, telegram to Vienna that Germany 'must decline to be irresponsibly dragged into a world war'.[11]

It would, of course, be unreasonable to suggest that, on 4 August 1914, there still existed a serious possibility of arresting the fatal avalanche of events. Goschen and Bethman-Hollweg were performing a Wagnerian duet, a cadenza to a civilisation that had already entered its irreversible agony. Nevertheless each was faithfully representing the illusions of his government and their exchange constitutes a revealing example of cant in its most high-minded, most plausible and most pernicious form. Neither was lying: each was selecting certain aspects of the situation and emphasising these at the expense of others omitted. Both preferred metaphors and abstractions to any analysis of concrete cause and effect: naval dispositions, the Schlieffen Plan, the movements of mobilising armies. Only Bethman-Hollweg's final question hints at any awareness of the real issues at stake, issues undreamt of in London, where the Foreign Secretary had already told an ignorant House of Commons that 'if we are engaged in war, we shall suffer but little more than we shall suffer if we stand aside'.[12]

It is, perhaps, in its sublimation of human suffering, in its abstraction of the argument from the details of death and destruction, from the tedious particulars of profit and loss, that the most characteristic feature of cant is to be detected. When a situation is described or a course of action explained or a result predicted, not in concrete, material and ultimately verifiable terms, but by the use of abstractions or metaphors calculated to evoke a particular emotional response, there is usually cause to suspect the presence of cant.

Compare, for instance, these two statements:

Our strategic policy must continue to be the deterrence of a deliberate nuclear attack against the United States or its allies... what level of potential destruction would have to be achieved to maintain that deterrence?... In the case of the Soviet Union, I would judge that a capability on our part to destroy, say, one-fifth to one-fourth of her population and one-half of her industrial capacity would serve as an effective deterrent.[13]

In recent months attacks on South Vietnam were stepped up. Thus it became necessary to increase our response and make attacks by air. This is not a change of purpose. It is a change in what we believe that purpose required. We do this in order to slow down aggression.

We do this to increase the confidence of the brave people of South Vietnam who have bravely borne this brutal battle for so many years and with so many casualties.

And we do this to convince the leaders of North Vietnam – and all who seek to share their conquest – of a simple fact:

We will not be defeated. We will not grow tired. We will not withdraw, either openly or under the cloak of a meaningless agreement.

We know that air attacks alone will not accomplish all these purposes. But it is our best and prayerful judgement that they are a necessary part of the surest road to peace.[14]

Both these predictions regarding the deterrent effects of aerial bombardment are representative extracts from much longer public statements, each of which is throughout its length stylistically consistent with the portion quoted. The first is always concrete, dispassionate and factual: the objective is assumed, not argued, and the means of its attainment are described with cold precision. The second is a prolonged appeal for emotional approval, in which the objective is described in abstract and metaphorical terms, but nothing whatever is said concerning the nature of the 'air attacks' or their expected results. Even an opponent of the policies of Mr McNamara (author of the first statement) could scarcely accuse him of cant in their expression, but it would be difficult for anyone to acquit President Johnson (author of the second) of the same charge, particularly in his choice of the epithet 'prayerful' in justifying his decision to bomb North Vietnam.

It may be objected that rhetorical utterance is a necessary element in political leadership and that public speeches on urgent and important topics can not be expected to meet the fastidious criteria of the man of letters or to survive the retrospective judgment of the historian. But the mode of expression always reveals the cast of thought and it is probably more than a coincidence that, even without the assistance of prayer, Mr McNamara's judgment has so far proved more accurate than President Johnson's. Someone who predicts that specific actions will have concrete results is more likely to be right than someone who talks, and thinks, in terms of 'the surest road to peace'.

Unfortunately it is easier to multiply instances of the use of cant than to arrive at a precise and generally acceptable definition of its characteristics. It may be true that cant usually entails an abstract and metaphorical appeal to emotion, but not all such exhortations are necessarily to be classed as cant. Consider, for instance, the following passage of rhetoric:

Now that I have taken up my office as Prime Minister and Minister of Defence I look back to our meetings in Rome and feel a desire to speak words of goodwill to you as Chief of the Italian nation across what seems to be a swiftly-widening gulf. Is it too late to stop a river of blood from flowing between the British and Italian peoples? We can no doubt inflict grievous injuries upon one another and maul each other cruelly and darken the Mediterranean with our strife. If you so decree, it must be so; but I declare that I have never been the enemy of Italian greatness, nor ever at heart the foe of the Italian law-giver. It is idle to predict the course of the great battles now raging in Europe, but I am sure that whatever may happen on the Continent England will go on to the end, even quite alone, as we have done before, and I believe with some assurance that we shall be aided in increasing measure by the United States and, indeed, by all the Americas.[15]

Here indeed is hyperbole and a luxuriance of emotive abstraction. Yet analysis of this florid language reveals its close concern with the practical situation – the danger of war with Italy; an objective assessment of its mutual disadvantages; a realistic admission that the outcome of the campaign in France was uncertain and an equally realistic forecast that Britain would continue the fight in the confident expectation of American assistance. Above all, there is an entire absence of any one-sided appeal to moral principles. Even the denial of personal enmity – perhaps the nearest approach to cant – is historically tenable and, in the Head of a new Government, relevant. Otherwise the arguments adduced for the avoidance of war rely entirely on considerations of common interest and, with some alteration of language, could equally well have been drafted for Mussolini by his own officials.

Conversely, when the sober Mr McNamara turns his attention to Vietnam, he abandons his usual endeavour dispassionately to assess and, wherever possible, to quantify the capacities and intention of his opponents, for a one-sided appeal to abstraction:

> We find ourselves engaged in a conflict with North Vietnam and its South Vietnamese supporters to preserve the principle that political change must not be brought about by externally directed violence and military force.[16]

The language may be cool, but the cant is unmistakable. Even if the principle were valid, even if it had been consistently observed by the United States, even if the adverb 'externally' could properly be applied to North Vietnam, that conflict has seen no monopoly of 'externally directed violence and military force'. Larger questions have seldom been more concisely begged.

Indeed, although the applications of cant are infinite and its characteristics various, it may perhaps be most easily identified by the preference shown by its practitioners for explaining their actions in terms of their own motives and principles. It is a common observation of everyday life that actions of benevolence seldom require or receive any moral justification. The man who explains his motives and invokes his principles does so to excuse himself for disobliging you. In international exchanges it is in their disputes that governments endeavour: 'to make up what was wanting in the justice of their cause . . . by a cant and sophistical way of expression'.[17]

The full implications of this practice are often missed by those who seize only on the plentiful evidence of inconsistency in the proclamation of principles. On 24 August 1939, for instance, the British Prime

Minister told an acquiescent House of Commons that:

> We want to see established an international order based upon
> mutual understanding and mutual confidence, and we cannot build
> such an order unless it conforms to certain principles which are
> essential to the establishment of confidence and trust. Those prin-
> ciples must include the observance of international undertakings
> when they have once been entered into . . . if despite our efforts to
> find the way of peace . . . [18] we find ourselves forced to embark upon
> a struggle which is bound to be fraught with suffering and misery
> for all mankind and the end of which no man can foresee, if that
> should happen, we shall be fighting for the preservation of those
> principles of which I have spoken, the destruction of which would
> involve the destruction of all possibility of peace and security for
> the peoples of the world.[19]

This Prime Minister was Neville Chamberlain, who, as Chancellor
of the Exchequer, had earlier reminded the House that:

> When we are told that contracts must be kept sacred, and that we
> must on no account depart from the obligations we have under-
> taken, it must not be forgotten that we have other obligations and
> responsibilities, obligations not only to our own countrymen but to
> many millions of human beings throughout the world, whose
> happiness or misery may depend upon how far the fulfillment of
> these obligations is insisted upon on the one side and met on the
> other.[20]

If any of the thirty million human beings who perished in that
struggle were ever aware of the principles on which they died, some of
them might have preferred Chamberlain's earlier pronouncement to
his second thoughts, but, if they had realised that this heartwarming
elevation of human happiness over the sanctity of contracts was no
more than an excuse for ceasing repayment of an American loan, they
might have been excused the cynical view that the element of cant was
equally redolent in each, as it was in all the other declarations of
principle made by every one of the leaders of the warring nations. If
the examples quoted in these pages have been selected primarily from
English-speaking sources, it is not for any lack of corresponding
utterances in other languages. Cant is international, but English-

speaking readers need less convincing of its existence among foreigners.

But inconsistency, though a frequent characteristic, is no more a necessary attribute of cant than untruth, insincerity or rhetorical and inappropriate language. It is the invocation of principles and the attribution of motives that identifies cant and not the merits of either. The statesman who sincerely believes himself to be defending righteous action in a good cause is still guilty of cant if he is more concerned with his own virtue than with the predictable and concrete results of his action. In the thermo-nuclear age the old saying that the road to Hell is paved with good intentions has acquired a new and more frightening significance. As long as Russian and American rulers are actuated by calculation, we may hope to survive in the knowledge that 'it is now impossible for either the United States or the Soviet Union to achieve a meaningful victory over the other in a strategic nuclear exchange.'[21]

But, if principles are allowed to predominate over considerations of profit and loss, then the prospects for the human race are sombre indeed. Interest is a universal language and, properly comprehended, can lead men to compromise: principles divide them and, if pressed to their different conclusions, can only tend, through bewilderment and exasperation, to final disaster.[22]

The principles thus condemned are naturally those, whether ethical, ideological or religious, solely concerned with the intrinsic nature and quality of actions without regard to their likely results. There is no necessarily pernicious element in those principles of political conduct intended only to assist statesmen in the making of advantageous choices or in predicting the consequences of their decisions. Theory has its proper place in politics as long as it is rooted in the real world and firmly directed towards practical objectives. It is the principles which justify means, not by their rationally expected results, but by the motives of those who select them, that are to be avoided.

It is because cant is the language of such principles that it is dangerous – and would still be dangerous even if the principles professed were intrinsically valid and consistently applied. These principles and their cant are the expression of irresponsibility: the negation of that ancient maxim of English law that reasonable men may be presumed to intend the natural consequences of their acts. Once motives are allowed to excuse results, foreign policy is divorced from the rule of reason and leads inevitably, but on an immeasurably larger and more disastrous scale, to the crime passionel. If Scottish readers will forgive the solecism of preferring the rhythm to the original sense, it is worth recalling that one of the earliest instances of the word in the *Oxford English Dictionary* is the profoundly symbolic phrase: 'cant men and cruel'. From the malign influence of such men may reason, cynicism and the dispassionate analysis of the probable deliver us all.

10 Hong Kong: a Base Without a Fleet

> No Englishman can land at Hong Kong without feeling a
> thrill of pride for his nationality. Here is the furthermost link
> in the chain of fortresses which, from Spain to China, girdles
> half the globe.
>
> Curzon[1]

When have pacifists, one wonders, done as much harm as the naive
patriot? Hong Kong never was a fortress. Admiral Seymour, who
commanded the China Squadron when Curzon wrote those words in
1898, was blunt: 'it is fortified of course, but neither in its defences
nor its garrison could it pretend to stand a siege – the reply I suppose
being, that we hope to command the sea'.[2]

HONG KONG ACQUIRED

That was a reasonable aspiration when Hong Kong, 'a barren island
with hardly a house upon it',[3] was first acquired in 1842 by the Treaty
of Nanking. This instrument, since known in China as 'The First
Unequal Treaty', had terminated the naval war of 1841, itself fought
to enforce the right of British merchants to trade with China. This
commerce was over a century old – John Duncan, eldest brother of
the Admiral who won the battle of Camperdown, died in 1750 aboard
an East Indiaman in the Chinese harbour of Whampoa – but had
always been subject to vexatious Chinese restrictions. In 1839 the
British Superintendent of Trade declared 'There can be neither safety
nor honour – until Her Majesty's flag flies on these coasts in a secure
position.'[4] In spite of much reluctance in London he got his way and,
from 1843, Hong Kong was a British colony, a trading entrepôt and a
base for naval operations, whether in renewed war with China, against
pirates or in the protection of British subjects deep in the heart of

China. For another century British warships would ascend the great rivers of China, trade would flourish and Rear-Admiral Yangtse earn his arrogant title. Admiral Seymour was equally correct in his view that 'the importance of Hong Kong to our squadron and our trade can hardly be overrated'.[5]

By the end of the nineteenth century, however, his 'hope to command the sea' had more precarious foundations. Kowloon had been ceded in 1860 (another 'unequal treaty') and the New Territories leased in 1898 (though some assistance from HMS FAME was needed before that 'unequal treaty' could be implemented). The colony of Hong Kong now comprised the original island of that name, 3½ square miles on the mainland (Kowloon), Stonecutters Island (all owned in full sovereignty) and 355 square miles of leased territory on the mainland and in 235 small islands. British rule no longer depended on the 66 warships deployed in 1861, but on three battleships, three armoured cruisers and seven unarmoured. Naturally there were also gunboats to ascend those rivers which China was still not organised to defend, but the China Squadron of the Royal Navy no longer had the strength to withstand the potential challenge in Pacific waters of the Franco-Russian Alliance – nine battleships and 20 cruisers in 1901.

ANGLO-JAPANESE ALLIANCE AND HONG KONG

This discrepancy was the main motive for the First Anglo-Japanese Alliance of 1902, which also saved the British Government the expense of the new docks and coaling facilities at Hong Kong which a larger fleet would have demanded. The colony was a better base than ever for British trade with China and its naval protection – it had sustained the expedition of 1900 for the relief of the besieged legations at Peking – but it was no longer supported by a sufficient fleet. In spite of the partial withdrawal imposed in 1899 by the needs of the Boer War, that fleet was at least substantial. In 1905, for instance, there were five battleships and five armoured cruisers. The Second Anglo-Japanese Alliance of 1905 and the crushing Japanese naval victory at Tsushima were followed by the withdrawal of the five battleships. The Russian Navy no longer existed, the French were now friendly and the battleships were needed in the Narrow Seas. But the security of Hong Kong – and of the British Empire from India to Australia – henceforth depended on the Anglo-Japanese Alliance. In 1910 Japan had 11 battleships, 13 armoured cruisers and 17 protected cruisers. There was, the British Government concluded in 1911, no other threat to Hong Kong.

The Third Anglo-Japanese Alliance of 1911 was accordingly not directed against anyone in particular, though Britain tried to make clear that it would not apply against the United States, now second to Japan as a Pacific naval power. It was intended, in London at least, to allow Britain to concentrate her naval strength in the North Sea. In 1912 the China Squadron was accordingly reduced – gunboats always excepted – to two armoured cruisers and two unarmoured.

This was manifestly unequal to the German squadron based on Tsingtao: two heavy cruisers and three light, the ships more modern and – as the disastrous battle of Coronel was to prove – the crews better trained.

In 1913, therefore, the Admiralty reinforced the China Squadron by sending out HMS TRIUMPH, a 12,000 ton pre-dreadnought battleship purchased from Chile in 1903 when the Russo-Japanese War of 1904–5 seemed imminent. Even so, in March 1914, Winston Churchill, then First Lord of the Admiralty, pointed out that the safety of, not merely Hong Kong, but Australia and New Zealand depended on the Anglo-Japanese Alliance.

It was thus a prudent precaution, on 3 August 1914, for the British Ambassador in Tokyo to inform the Japanese Government that 'if hostilities spread to Far East, and an attack on Hong Kong or Wei-hai-wei [another British naval base in China] were to take place, we should rely on their support'.[6] The Japanese gave their promise the next day and this was soon followed by agreement to undertake responsibility for all naval patrolling and commerce protection north of the Equator.

This was all the more useful, in spite of the presence of a battle-cruiser and two modern cruisers in Australian waters, because TRIUMPH had just been paid off to undergo a long refit at Hong Kong. Heroic efforts – and the transfer of crews from demobilised gunboats – enabled her to take part that autumn in the capture of Tsingtao by Japanese forces (the first clear Allied victory over Germany anywhere in that war), but the British command of the sea predicated by Admiral Seymour was otherwise slow to appear. The Japanese Navy was required to escort New Zealand troop convoys, to operate as far as Aden and, in 1917, to send four destroyers to the Mediterranean. In that war Hong Kong was a useful base, but not for a sufficient fleet. The colony depended, as did British power and influence east of Suez, on the alliance with Japan.

In 1917, admittedly, HMS SUFFOLK was despatched from Hong Kong to Vladivostok to initiate the British response to the Bolshevik revolution in Russia. Even so, the Japanese navy got there first.

The lessons were not altogether disregarded in London. In 1920 Lord Jellicoe, despatched on an Imperial tour, predicted eventual war with Japan and recommended the creation of a Far Eastern Fleet (25 per cent of it to be financed by Australia and New Zealand) of eight battleships, eight battle-cruisers and four aircraft carriers.

BETWEEN THE WARS

Nobody agreed. Nor was the obvious alternative – continuation of the Anglo-Japanese Alliance – accepted. Fear of an Anglo-American naval race (the US Navy went on planning war with Britain until June 1939) prompted first the Washington Four Power Treaty of 1921, whch terminated the Anglo-Japanese Alliance without providing any alternative beyond mutual consultation; then the Washington Naval Treaty of 1922, which conceded naval preponderance in the Pacific to Japan and prohibited the fortification of Hong Kong. A divided and reluctant British Government, against the advice of the Australian, British and New Zealand Prime Ministers, had concluded that it was better to risk Japanese hostility than American, even though American assistance was rightly regarded as less reliable than Japanese. Britain was henceforth on her own in the Pacific. So was Hong Kong.

It proved its value during the turbulence that devastated China throughout the period between the two World Wars. In 1932 17 Chinese cities contained substantial British communities. All but two could be reached by warships. These were so often required – to protect British subjects from violence which the Chinese authorities were unable or unwilling to prevent – that the Royal Navy sent a circular to British Consuls urging them not to interfere with the training season by calling for gunboats between March and October. Sometimes even a gunboat was not enough. Cruisers could reach Chingkiang, 200 miles from the sea, and in 1932 a cruiser squadron was sent to Shanghai to protect the International Concession there, which had attracted nine British warships and an expeditionary force of 13,000 men in 1927. For all these activities – and there was never a year in which the gunboats were idle – Hong Kong was the main base, as it was for the China Fleet (the nomenclature varied). In 1933 this comprised five cruisers, one light carrier, two small cruisers, nine destroyers, 12 to 15 submarines and numerous sloops and gunboats. Of these only the submarines were expected to confront the Japanese Navy in war (their role being to defend Hong Kong for 48 days until the main fleet reached Singapore from home waters). The exigencies of violent peace provided ample employment for the remainder.

This period also witnessed a further growth in the population and commercial importance of Hong Kong, as immigrants poured in from the troubled mainland and trading posts were withdrawn from the interior. Even Shanghai, long the economic centre of Western enterprise in China, its rich International Concession guarded by British and other foreign soldiers, began to seem less secure than the Colony.

JAPAN, CHINA AND HONG KONG

The difference, unfortunately, was only relative. Japanese denunciation of the Washington Treaty having removed the ban on the fortification of Hong Kong, the Gindrinkers Defence Line was constructed in the New Territories during 1937, but the Chiefs of Staff in London, conscious of the growing threat in Europe from Germany and Italy, now saw little hope of holding Hong Kong in war. The strength of the China Squadron had risen to six cruisers, one light carrier, 10 destroyers and the largest concentration of submarines (17) outside home waters, but the time needed for the main fleet to reach Singapore was now estimated at 180 days. British relations with Japan had progressively deteriorated ever since the termination of the Alliance, not least during Japan's war with China. That war had also given Japan cause to resent the existence of Hong Kong: in 1938, it was estimated, 75 per cent of China's imported war material passed through the Colony. By the end of that year, however, Japanese troops had extended their advance into the area of mainland China adjacent to the New Territories.

There is no need to dwell on the rest of the melancholy story: the rejection (in May 1939) of the Chinese offer of 20,000 troops for the defence of Hong Kong; the progressive reduction of the China Squadron; Churchill's decision in January 1941 that the Colony was indefensible; the surrender on December 25, after a brief defence by six battalions, one destroyer, four gunboats, eight motor torpedo boats and five obsolete aircraft. The decisive events had occurred elsewhere.

> Considering the present state of affairs in the East, I thought it better to send you a Vice-Admiral in a line-of-battle ship; so that the full impression might be produced [of] – our fixed determination to uphold the predominance of our power, which is so much founded on opinion in your Eastern regions.[7]

That was what Churchill decided in August 1941, but the words are those of Sir James Graham in 1832. The passage of a century had destroyed the original validity of the concept. When Admiral Phillips went down with PRINCE OF WALES and REPULSE, the process begun by the withdrawal of Admiral Noel's battleships from the China Station in 1905, and only postponed during the twenty years of the Anglo-Japanese Alliance, reached its climax. The British Empire in the East had been created by British sea power and could not survive the collapse of that power, even if an artificial existence could be maintained for a few fragments for many years.

COMMUNIST CHINA AND HONG KONG

One of the most unexpected of these surviving fragments is Hong Kong. In February 1945, while the Colony was still in Japanese hands, Roosevelt had urged its return to China. Even when Admiral Harcourt arrived with the battleship ANSON and the carriers INDOMITABLE and VENERABLE to accept the Japanese surrender, there must have been many who wondered whether this would prove more than a transitory ceremony. There was no longer a hostile fleet to fear, but war-time experience had demonstrated the vulnerability of Hong Kong to attack from the mainland. This was greatly increased by the post-war expansion of the Colony's population and the development of the New Territories to provide the Colony with its airport, water, electricity, industry and agricultural land. Local defence was inconceivable; Britain could no longer fight a war with China nor deter her from starting one; the United States, even at the zenith of their imperial ardour, refused to include Hong Kong among the territories covered by the South-East Asia Treaty Organisation of

1954. Hong Kong has for thirty years been as dependent on Chinese tolerance as once it was on Japanese.

This tolerance has itself been surprising. Early omens were scarcely auspicious: Communist ascendancy in China; the AMETHYST incident of 1949; British and Chinese troops fighting one another in the Korean War. British recognition of the new regime in 1950 was not reciprocated before 1954 and only in 1972 did China agree to an exchange of ambassadors. That, incidentally, was also the year when China, newly admitted to the United Nations, asked that organisation to delete Hong Kong and Macao from the list of internationally recognised colonial territories. Neither the state of Chinese relations with Britain nor the anti-colonial climate of international opinion seemed to offer Hong Kong much prospect of immunity. The Soviet Union, both before and after their own break with China, enjoyed needling Peking on the subject and the United States were at best indifferent.

Nevertheless, in contrast to Chinese belligerence over Taiwan and its off-shore islands, to the seizure of the Paracels, the fighting along the Soviet border, the interventions in Korea and Indo-China, the forceful fishery disputes with Japan, there has been only one incident that seriously disturbed the tranquillity of Hong Kong. In 1966–7, during China's cultural revolution, when the British Embassy in Peking was burned, there were riots in the Colony. Whether or not these were directly instigated from China is uncertain, but they were not very serious and their suppression by the Colonial Government, though criticised by Chinese propaganda, did not attract Chinese interference.

Naturally the Chinese Government have never departed from their expressed view that Hong Kong is Chinese territory illegally acquired by 'unequal treaties', but they have never attempted to enforce their claim by any of the many means available to them. Even water, for instance, still has to be imported from China, to say nothing of the Colony's dependence on trade with China.

PROSPERITY AND POPULATION IN HONG KONG

This surprising immunity has permitted a phenomenal growth in the population and prosperity of Hong Kong. The income per head of its more than five million inhabitants is the third highest in the Far East

after Japan and Singapore – US$3000 in 1978. Overcrowding – a
million immigrants have arrived from China since 1950 – is naturally
formidable (25,000 people per square kilometre in urban areas) but
has been alleviated by a massive public housing programme. By 1977
government expenditure on social services was eight times greater than
it had been a decade earlier. Perhaps the most striking feature is that
Hong Kong, having lived on transit trade for more than a century,
now manufactures 80 per cent of its exports.

Yet it remains a colony and its people (98 per cent of them Chinese)
elect representatives only to the Urban Council, the unofficial
majorities in the Executive and Legislative Councils comprising only
nominated members. It is, of course, rather a peculiar kind of colony,
enjoying far more autonomy in practice than it does in theory. The
obstacle to full self-government, indeed to independence, is not in
London but in Peking. The Chinese Government, which reiterated in
September 1982 their intention of recovering Hong Kong 'when
conditions are ripe',[8] would much rather tolerate an unrecovered
colony on their doorstep than another Taiwan. This is well understood
in Hong Kong, where a public opinion poll in May–June 1982
suggested that 69 per cent of the inhabitants favoured the maintenance
of the *status quo*, and few believed in the possibility of independence.[9]

But why should China tolerate, even provisionally, any alternative
to Chinese rule and sovereignty? Her opportunities, compared to
those of Argentina, are as varied and overwhelming as the obstacles
are insignificant. Naturally the Chinese have never offered an official
reply to that question, but the answer usually accepted elsewhere is
economic. China is supposed to earn nearly half her foreign exchange
from and through Hong Kong – an estimated £4 billion in 1982. The
Chinese Government – so it is assumed – realise that much of this
would be lost if Hong Kong were to be integrated into the Communist
system. To restore Chinese sovereignty without such integration
might, however, pose political problems. Even in the vast population
of China there could be repercussions if five million people were given
treatment sufficiently privileged to sustain the present economic
dynamism of Hong Kong.

'When conditions are ripe' may accordingly mean when China has
developed alternative means of earning enough foreign exchange, or
when Chinese leaders have found the compromise they are believed to
be seeking, at least for regional application, between political con-
formity and economic enterprise. The problem will become
increasingly urgent as 1997 approaches, the year when the lease of the

New Territories expires. It is hard to imagine how any Chinese leadership could justify – to themselves, their people or the outside world – a renewal of the lease. With no prospect of renewal, however, special and early incentives would be needed to prevent a flight from Hong Kong of the capital and at least some of the people now laying golden eggs for China. Without the New Territories Hong Kong is not remotely viable.

HONG KONG'S VALUE TO BRITAIN

Britain's dilemma will become even more acute. Hong Kong is fast losing its value to Britain. There is neither a fleet to use the base nor any purpose for such a fleet to serve. Admittedly Hong Kong is more than ever vital to trade with China, but much of the profit from that trade now stays in Hong Kong, whose own manufacturing capabilities also offer unwelcome competition to ailing British industries. In any case, the importance to Britain of the China trade has always been exaggerated: in 1976 British exports to China were a quarter of those to Finland. Hong Kong no longer supports sterling and in 1976 kept only 20 per cent of its reserves in that currency. Individual Britons still find careers and profits in Hong Kong and some British firms do good business there, but the advantage to the British people of retaining the colony is problematic. Even the opportunities for 'China-watching' which it offers to the flourishing and cosmopolitan intelligence community are of more interest to the United States than to Britain.[10]

Admittedly, unlike Gibraltar, Hong Kong imposes no direct burdens on the British economy. The political costs are more significant. British rule in Hong Kong makes relations with China more difficult, but, as its continuation depends on Chinese tolerance, also gives China more leverage on British policy, both in the Colony and outside. During the Vietnam War, for instance, the need to allow Hong Kong registered ships to supply North Vietnam while denying to the Seventh Fleet the opportunity for rest and recreation in Hong Kong caused friction in Anglo-American relations. In the late seventies the influx of Vietnamese refugees into Hong Kong (70,000 in 1979) imposed on the British Government an obligation, which might not have been accepted without the colonial responsibility, to receive some of them in the British Isles.

Immigration, indeed, is the main problem of the immediate future. Without attempting any analysis of the precise national status of the inhabitants of Hong Kong, it must be accepted that many of them have a claim to British protection, if not always to any form of British citizenship. They are also, it is generally agreed, an intensely migratory population. Most of them came to Hong Kong, or remained in Hong Kong, because the opportunities for material reward seemed greater there than in mainland China, which is still the dominant source of personal relationships and instinctive sympathies. In 1978, admittedly, it was estimated that 59 per cent of the population had been born in Hong Kong, but neither the Colony nor British rule are regarded as the natural focus of loyalty. Most, as earlier suggested, prefer the *status quo*; most, if the choice is forced upon them, would probably accept Chinese rule. But there could be a substantial minority, as 1997 approaches, who would again want to wander where the grass was greener. It is unlikely, in the absence of an altogether improbable renaissance of the British economy, that Britain would be their preferred destination. But it might seem the most accessible: a country with an arguable obligation to receive them. In the nineties immigration from Hong Kong could constitute a major problem for British politicians.

RN COMMITMENT AND HONG KONG'S FUTURE

Meanwhile immigration into Hong Kong provides Britain's last naval task in the Far East. Four thousand illegal immigrants were arrested in the first four months of 1982 and many Chinese, as well as Vietnamese, come by sea. The strength of the Hong Kong Marine Police is to be substantially increased from the present level of 2000 men and 50 vessels to cope with the inshore aspects of combatting illegal immigration, smuggling and piracy. The half dozen Royal Navy patrol craft and two hovercraft operating outside territorial waters are to be supplemented (perhaps replaced) by five new, specially built patrol vessels. Critics of this decision complain that these new ships will be needlessly large, sophisticated and expensive for their possibly ephemeral tasks. Are these ships actually intended for other uses once the Royal Navy ceases to be responsible for Hong Kong? As 75 per cent of the cost is being met by the Colonial Government, such a transfer might not be altogether easy.

It is, however, the least of the problems requiring resolution in the confidential talks on the future of Hong Kong which began in Peking in October 1982.[11] Although Chinese officials have been at pains to disseminate an impression of benevolence, the five million people now supported by what was once 'a barren island with hardly a house upon it' can only choose between emigrating and adapting themselves to whatever destiny may be prescribed for them by the rulers of nearly a billion of their fellow Chinese. If this future includes a degree of autonomy, so much the better, but Hong Kong never was a fortress; no longer enjoys effective protection and has largely ceased to be a colony without becoming a nation. For Britain the story will end as it began – as it was bound to end once Hong Kong became a base without a fleet – in an unequal treaty.

11 The Useful Art of International Relations

The title declares the theme: that utility should be the criterion for the study of international relations, which is a functional art.

This concept naturally implies a reciprocal, even a causal connection between the study of international relations and its practical conduct. As will later be argued, this connection can and does manifest itself in many different ways. In the United States, for instance, scholars have frequently become practitioners. In the Soviet Union the relevant academic institutions make important contributions to the formation and exposition of official policy. Many countries demand a specifically professional element in the academic training of their prentice diplomats. These are by no means the only ways in which the subject can be useful, but they are perhaps the most obvious.

Such easy arguments are not available in Britain, where the teaching of international relations and its practical conduct have long proceeded in an independence that may once have been dignified, but now often approaches the absurd. In the two previous decades, for instance, successive British governments commissioned three separate reports, each intended as a more or less independent check on the views of those directly concerned, on Overseas Representation. Each embodied a more or less portentous pronouncement on the nature of Britain's international relations and foreign policy. Although relevant professors are traditionally selected as members of such governmental commissions, Britain's faculties of international relations were represented on none of these enquiries. The nearest approach was the appointment of the late Andrew Shonfield, an economist but then also director of studies at Chatham House, as a member of the Duncan Committee (1968–9). This governmental disdain for professors of international relations seems to have been reciprocated. Although each commission attracted a remarkable variety of witnesses, no university teacher of international relations gave evidence to the

Plowden Committee (1964), only three to the Duncan Committee and one to the CPRS (1977). By a curious coincidence these four were all Australians. 'Gentlemen in England, now abed', where were you? The entire burden of representing the 'discipline' in Britain was borne by Chatham House.

For British readers, therefore, some preliminary analysis is needed of a concept often taken for granted in other countries. Not only do objections exist, but they come from more sources than one.

Utility and function will furnish the meat of the argument, but this has to begin by recognising the existence of different conceptions of the academic nature of international relations. Some views, of course, are self-refuting.

> As a focus of study, the nation-state is no different from the atom or the single cell organism. Its patterns of behaviour, idiosyncratic traits, and internal structure are as amenable to the process of formulating and testing hypotheses as are the characteristics of the electron or the molecule.[1]

The idea of international relations as an exact science has always been repugnant to common sense, but it is convenient to have so concise a self-exposure of its fallacy. Much may be borrowed, even by the dangerous way of analogy, from the natural sciences, but not reliable knowledge. 'The fundamental principle of scientific observation is that all human beings are interchangeable as observers.' This 'restricts scientific information about the external world to those observations on which independent observers can agree'.[2] Apply this to international relations, in Moscow and Peking, as well as New York and Lancaster, and what is left?

Nevertheless, the scientific approach does not offer the only pathway to knowledge and truth. Should not these be accepted, in international relations no less than in history or in the establishment of classical texts, as the proper goals of academic endeavour? Many respectable scholars do see their subject – the term 'discipline' has disagreeable overtones – as existing in its own right, independent of outside influence and heedless of practical consequences, an open field for investigation and a source of unbounded speculation.

This is by no means an ignoble ambition. Its feasibility and its compatibility with the two criteria initially suggested – utility and function – will have to be examined subsequently. At this early stage of the argument two comments suggest themselves.

The first is that international relations differs in two important respects from many other subjects of academic enquiry. It is a continuing process and it is one inseparable from human choice. The historian, the palaeontologist, the classicist are studying material that already exists – even if unsuspected – in its final state. They may make new discoveries, offer fresh interpretations, apply novel methods, but their subject matter is not in constant evolution. The existence, the fate or the conflicting interests of the human race are not specially relevant to the work of the astronomer, the pure mathematician, the theoretical physicist. In international relations, on the other hand, the scholar is not merely at the mercy of the morning's headlines: he is also, and more intimately than Einstein ever imagined, a part of the process he is observing. It is admittedly possible – there are some notorious examples – to study international relations without regard to its actual conduct. It is more difficult to select a subject for investigation, to adopt a method, to decide on an approach – let alone to express an opinion – without making a political choice. The personal bias and the culture-bound assumptions that leap to the eye in the traditional writers are equally discernible in those who seek objectivity in their computers. Not everyone would endorse David Easton's view that 'behavioural science conceals an ideology based upon empirical conservatism',[3] but the permeation by ideology of the study of international relations is as obvious as the identification of specific odours is sometimes controversial. Politics, of which international relations is a branch, cannot be sanitised by calling it political science.

International relations, alas, is not an abstract subject, nor can it be the preserve of scholars caring only for the advancement of learning and the establishment of academic standards. It is not a fine art, in which potential influence might be irrelevant to the intrinsic merits of poem or picture. There are none of the pure revelations, the fleeting certainties of the natural sciences. Architecture, landscape gardening and cookery are all examples of the need to marry the creative vision to the practical requirements of everyday life before any achievement can be claimed.

An even better example of the useful art – only the abnormally healthy could call it a science – is medicine: at its most successful a blend of training, research, clinical experience and instinctive perception. It resembles international relations in the diversity of its sources of knowledge, in the constant evolution of the subject, in the frequency with which methods are accepted before their theoretical justification can be ascertained, in its widespread and profound implications for ordinary human lives. There are also important differences. There of them go to the heart of the present argument.

The principle of utility, for instance, in widely accepted. Research or administration may create worlds of their own, but few of the doctors thus engaged would care to repudiate as the ultimate test of their activities some contribution to the ability of practitioners to prolong life or relieve pain. Medicine is also functional: it cannot be studied or taught without the involvement of both practitioners and patients. Finally, medicine is professional. Whether theoretical or practical, it is dominated by men and women who have undergone a similar basic training, who are familiar with a common vocabulary, who share at least a minimum of received opinions and assumptions.

It is hard for scholars of international relations to prevent their subject from being functional. Their data, however abstract the treatment, are drawn from the real world of actions and events. The mere classification and ordering of this data, let alone its interpretation and any conclusions that may be deduced from it, have implications that can scarcely be concealed – in the manner of doctors restricting the circulation of their cases-notes – from all but other scholars. And even these may become actors. Bundy, Rostow, Kissinger, and Brzezinski followed one another in the White House. Ideas will out and may ultimately influence actions.

A brief essay is no place for extended analysis of this influence, often unintended or indirect: Mahan and Kaiser Wilhelm II;[4] Houston Stewart Chamberlain and Hitler;[5] Barbara Tuchman and President Kennedy[6] are random examples; but it would not be hard to document a diplomatic parallel to Keynes's celebrated dictum that 'practical men, who believe themselves to be quite exempt from any intellectual influences, are usually the slaves of some defunct economist'.[7]

Unfortunately Keynes went on to say that 'madmen in authority, who hear voices in the air, are distilling their frenzy from some academic scribbler of a few years back'.[8] It is probably this nightmare vision which is responsible for the marked reluctance of scholars in international relations to accept the principle of utility as a criterion for the conduct of their studies. Useful to whom, they ask, and for what purpose? Such questions are naturally most pointed in private discussion, but the underlying attitude surfaces even in print. Philip Reynolds, for instance, professor of Politics at the University of Lancaster, argued in 1975 that 'the activity of theorizing – will not solve immediate policy problems. It will not offer ways of determining the "right action" to take in a particular situation.' So far, reluctant agreement is possible. But he adds: 'some would say that is all to the good'. That last sentence would be odd, even perverse, if it were addressed to students of medicine. Yet Michael Shackleton of the Open University quotes it as an argument against students of international politics and foreign policy entering the Diplomatic Service.[9] Both comments may have been frivolously intended, but both can be seen as symptoms of that endemic British disease: academics shrinking into the womb of 'pure' research and practitioners scorning 'theoretical' training. In other branches of learning that divorce is partly responsible for the decline of Britain in the last hundred years. Its disadvantages in the precarious present require little emphasis.

There is nevertheless something to be said on the other side. Scholarship, once harnessed to the ends of government, may be exploited for purposes repugnant to the academic community, if not always to the individual scholars concerned. Academic involvement in the formation or the exposition of policy during the Vietnam War, a process not confined to Americans alone, caused much retrospective heart-searching. It was not only the personal contribution of scholars that was questioned, but the influence exerted by their theories on practitioners. Professor Deutsch, for instance, lamented that:

the concepts of . . . 'totalitarianism' and its alleged opposite the 'free world' in an allegedly unending 'cold war'; the notions of the 'balance of power', the 'vacuum of power', and the 'domino effect' all these have turned out to be largely chaotic and unverifiable in theory, and sometimes deadly and disastrous in practice.[10]

He drew the conclusion that improved methods of study leading to better theories were required, but it could obviously be argued that scholars will best preserve their innocence if they not merely shun governmental employment, but flee the perils of a relevance that may be misapplied even if it is not actually mistaken.

This is not an acceptable argument. The study of international relations is not an innocent profession. It can do harm as well as good. The subject is a human condition and an activity widely pursued. Increased knowledge and deeper understanding may be desirable for their own sake, but can scarcely be imparted without some risk of influencing events as well as explaining them. The responsibility of scholars may be less direct, less inescapable, than that of politicians and diplomats, but it exists. It cannot be evaded, for instance, by specialising in what is apparently benevolent. Peace research sounds fine, but suppose it leads to the drawing of conclusions and the inculcation of attitudes that have the result of lulling public opinion into acquiescence in the slide to an otherwise avoidable global conflict? Nobody will ever prove – and it is not here asserted – that British pacifism caused the Second World War, but it is at least a more plausible candidate than British militarism in the 1930s. As for abstraction, sooner or later, that encounters a dilemma. Either it contains a message which someone will interpret, misinterpret or even misapply, or else it has no significance at all. And, if communication is renounced, it remains uncomfortably true that, in politics, abstention is also a choice. The attempt to remove significance is an incomplete abdication of responsibility. If the study of international relations is not useful, it can scarcely be represented as no more than a harmless hobby.

That brings us back to our earlier questions: useful to whom and for what purpose?

The ultimate answer is obvious: to practitioners. There is no point in a recipe if nobody is going to cook it. This does not mean that scholarship has to be prescriptive; that it should concentrate on topical issues or take too much account of current preconceptions; least of all that it should be geared to the needs of any particular category of practitioners. There will always be such scholars and their utility will often extend far beyond their chosen function. Mr Georgiy Arbatov, of the Soviet Institute of the United States and Canada, for instance, might be regarded as an extreme example of the functional scholar of international relations. His published output often conforms to all the conditions just specified as exceptional. Nevertheless, no serious student of international relations could afford to neglect his writings, his speeches or the occasional opportunities he offers for personal contact and discussion.

He has numerous Western equivalents. Because of differences in the organisation of society, their expository functions are at once less circumscribed and less authoritative, but they are nevertheless important. In Britain, in particular, educated public opinion is largely dependent on the academic community for the intelligent exposition of international problems and of British foreign policy. It would be agreeable, but unrealistic – *video meliora proboque deteriora sequor* – to imagine a British State Paper beginning:

without an understanding of the philosophical conception upon which specific actions were based, the actions themselves can neither be adequately understood nor fairly judged. This account of a year of intense action, therefore, properly begins with a brief review of the intellectual foundation on which those actions rest.[11]

The rare, the brief, the simplistic speeches of politicians are not supplemented even by the solid diet of Blue Books that was once customary. The nearest approach to a regular declaration of foreign policy is to be found in a few paragraphs of the annual *Statement on the Defence Estimates*. Of course, it cannot legitimately be demanded of the academic community that they should remedy the failings of ministers and officials, but we should all be grateful that some of them do. It is a useful function.

It is also essentially a by-product of the study of international relations. There is more to this branch of scholarship than the exposition of current affairs and more is needed to demonstrate the relevance to the subject as a whole of the principle of utility.

Similar arguments apply to the many tributaries that swell the main stream of international relations – and the following are only examples, not an exclusive list: history, geography, law, economics; the culture, politics, social structure and languages of particular countries; the disputed principles of sociology; arms control or strategy. Each of these can be individually useful, whether directly to practitioners or through the mediation of other scholars. Indeed, if they are to be reckoned at all in this argument, they have to be useful. None of them – whatever the University of Cambridge may think about history – is international relations. Each offers only a partial contribution. Many specialists, admittedly, have thought they could go further. Mackinder believed that his geographical expertise contained the key to political evolution and his prediction (in 1904) that 'Corea' would be one of the 'many bridge heads where the outside navies would support armies' against the 'vast continental resources' of Russia undoubtedly anticipated one interpretation of events by half a century.[12] The mastery of an unfamiliar language has led many a scholar to become first a political adviser, than an actual practitioner. Specialised studies in international relations are doubly utilitarian: in their own right and in their contribution to the essence of the subject. But it is against that essence, not its by-products or its constituents, that the principle of utility must be tested.

The essence of international relations as an academic subject, and the key to its utility, is theorising.

This is a proposition, at least as it is to be developed here, that will be generally disputed. Most practitioners will scorn it, because they agree with Professor Reynolds that 'theorizing – will not solve immediate policy problems', which they tend to regard as specific and uniquely important. The specialists will distrust it because their mastery of recondite knowledge seems to them to constitute the essential academic contribution to the problems of the often ignorant practitioner. Even the theorists will have major reservations. They are less ready than practitioners to regard any generalising principle as a theory. Some deny the title to any theories but their own. To others theory is still in gestation and unfit for profane eyes before the moment of its perfection. Many dislike the idea of practitioners picking and choosing among the available theoretical concepts only those which happen to suit them. Beneath all these particular doubts, half-buried by the controversies of two decades, lies the original bone of contention, the hope that once sustained some and still irritates others: that theory might one day establish an independent existence, that it could be 'proved'.

All these views are in some degree mistaken, but most of all that attributed to the practitioner. He may believe that he decides or recommends the decision of problems 'on their merits', but this is impossible. The mere identification of an event or a situation as constituting a problem, let alone a dispute, demands an initial preconception that what has happened is somehow of concern to his government. Lord Strang, for instance, gave the game away in his avowedly pragmatic argument that 'the number of ways in which the national interest can be damaged by foreign action is legion' so that 'to find the best way to meet each of them will call for an individual exercise, separately conducted'.[13]

Indeed it will and when the practitioner composes the traditional single sheet of paper, he will concentrate on the circumstantial nature of the problem and his specific proposals for action. If 'why' scrapes into an argument devoted to 'what' and 'how', it will be as a precedent or an analogy or one of those catchwords that are the shorthand expression of prevailing ideas – 'alliance solidarity', 'détente', 'human rights'. He will not even define the concept so important to practitioners and so distrusted by theorists: 'the national interest'. But the generalised principles thus briefly indicated will be quite as important in the decision as the facts of the case. Nor do ideas influence objectives alone. They creep into the choice of methods when these are labelled, whether by the 'hurrah-words' most dear to the government in power or by such superficially more objective epithets as 'linkage' or 'escalation' or 'signalling' or 'destabilising'. And even this language may conceal as many general ideas as it reflects. Practitioners are often intelligent, even if they are not always very systematic thinkers. Very few of their ideas are ever clearly articulated. As Lord Strang again remarked: 'Between Minister and officials who work together, there comes into existence a large area of common ground which all can take for granted and which does not need to be explained or demonstrated.'[14]

The common ground is fertilised from many sources, but few of the seeds are the original ideas of politicians and senior officials. They lack the time for fundamental or innovatory thinking. The sheer pace of decision-making in the contemporary conduct of international relations – and the general absence of any procedure for discriminating between the urgent and the important – make that impossible. The practitioner sees his task as being to apply the conventional wisdom to the solution of problems that are both concrete and pressing. Some practitioners may have contributed, in earlier years, to the formation of this conventional wisdom, but much of it comes from outside, from, using the word in its broadest and loosest sense, the theorists: not academics alone, but politicians out of office, journalists, officials with time on their hands, scribblers of every kind, cranks. Their influence tends to be slow, indirect, partial and even erratic. But it exists.

It is slow because men of power are reluctant to modify the ideas they acquired in the days of their youth. It is indirect, because these men do little serious reading and, if they are disposed to consider new ideas at all, prefer them to be presented in simplified form by people they consider to be either influential or reliable. It is partial because many ideas are offered in a form that is either incomprehensible or unlikely to attract their attention. It is erratic because the test applied by practitioners is not ultimate truth, but relevance.

The resulting impoverishment of the conventional wisdom – not only among politicians and diplomats but throughout the much wider circle of those who constitute or influence public opinion on international issues – is regrettable. In such a rapidly evolving subject received ideas are inherently prone to obsolescence and need constant challenge and renewal. This process is a natural task for scholars, whatever their subject, and the proper yardstick of utility in the study of international relations. This utility would be enhanced if some of the obstacles previously noted to the dissemination of new ideas could be overcome. Even the resistance of practitioners, however congenital, might be eroded by greater lucidity and relevance in the conceptual challenge to their often out-moded and usually over-simplified preconceptions.

This is easier said than done. Lucidity is not merely a gift of God: it can also be regarded as the enemy of precision. One eminent scholar, for instance, identified eleven separate meanings for that familiar expression: the balance of power. It is scarcely surprising that Professor Kaplan suggested that a scientific approach to international relations 'requires an articulated secondary language that permits reasonable precision and replicability'.[15] It is a thoroughly under-standable aspiration, recalling the earlier analogy with medicine, which has made greater progress in this direction. Doctors nevertheless need a measure of agreement among themselves on the relationship between symptoms and specific diseases before it is worth their while to describe either in words that often perplex their patients. No such agreement is likely in international relations, where the continued existence of different words for the same idea or of various meanings for the same word reflects incompatible political attitudes. Whether such familiar terms as 'balance of power' are employed or whether new words are coined, explanation will always be necessary if the full meaning is to be conveyed to the unconverted. The writer who saves himself this trouble by employing the shorthand of a specialised vocabulary does not merely burden his reader: he may also deter him by the political commitment implicit in his choice of words. The newer the idea, the simpler should be the language of its expression. Even for communication among scholars it would be hard to devise a better medium than the vernacular. For any wider audience 'it is a thing plainly repugnant' to discuss international relations 'in a tongue not understood of the people'.

It is nevertheless frequently attempted. American-Greek is a favourite choice, liberally salted with borrowings from the natural sciences and, when words fail the writer, with equations, graphs and flights of arrows. Such writing is often described, by its authors, as 'rigorous'. It is certainly hard to read and, therefore, less useful than it might be.

Relevance presents more difficult problems. Scholars are rightly resistant to the idea of restricting themselves to topical issues, nor would practitioners wish them to do so. On the other hand, the hankering, often discernible in the Foreign Office, for 'new ideas' from the academic community tends to be merely wistful. It is extremely difficult to devise a specific proposal that is novel, yet compatible with the objective facts and with existing preconceptions. The more the Foreign Office have tried, particularly since the late 1960s, to draw on the alternative wisdom of the academic community, the more often it has seemed that practitioners are asking the wrong kind of question. 'If I wanted to get there, I wouldn't start from here' may not be an immediately helpful answer, but it is more often the function of the scholar to modify the conventional wisdom than to reveal hitherto unsuspected opportunities for its practical application.

What practitioners need – even if only an enlightened minority actually want – is the constant renewal of their conceptual armoury: of the criteria which they have neither devised for themselves, nor thoroughly analysed, but which, often without knowing it, they use day by day. It is here that relevance becomes crucial, for politics is the art of the possible. Professor Goodwin rightly said that 'the academic's aim is to add to the understanding of policy choices, not to decide policy',[16] but understanding will not be increased if, for instance, the possibility of choice is denied or, at the other extreme, the constraints imposed on choice either by material circumstances or by received ideas are ignored. There is a scholarly place for determinist explanations of the international system; for the construction of ideal worlds; for abstract analysis of the psychology of decision-making; for every kind of theoretical speculation. Much of it may ultimately, and indirectly, prove its worth. But, if it does not add to the practitioner's understanding of the kind of choice likely to confront him, nor refine the conceptual tools he could actually apply in making such choices, then, to him, such theorising will be neither relevant nor fully useful.

The needs of the practitioner, it must again be emphasised, should not be narrowly construed as those of any particular category of practitioner. If individual scholars or groups of scholars or learned institutions devote their efforts to the intellectual enlightenment of the Foreign Office, they have chosen a relevant and useful task. But so they have if they are aiming at public opinion, at home or abroad, or at equipping their students with a better understanding of policy choices. In international relations we are all potential practitioners: the members of the Oxford Union whose notorious vote in 1933 may have encouraged British appeasement and German aggression; the young Americans whose smoking draft cards signalled the end for the United States in Vietnam; the anonymous voters whose referendum kept Britain in the European Economic Community; the Iranian students who humbled a Super Power.

Which of these might have benefited from a degree in international relations, and from which university, is a question which the present author resolutely declines to answer. But Gavrilo Princip, at least, was a plausible candidate for academic instruction in the understanding of choices. When interrogated about the death, on 28 June 1914, of the Archduke Franz Ferdinand von Österreich Este and his wife, Sophie Duchess of Hohenberg, he replied: 'My thought was therefore only on the success of the assassination; of some unfavourable consequence or other I had not thought at all'.[17]

To enhance the understanding of choices is naturally only the ultimate criterion for the study of international relations. Not every scholar will wish to theorise, nor to address himself directly to practitioners, actual or potential. Knowledge has to be accumulated and new methods of seeking it devised. If relevant theory is the essence, it must nevertheless be distilled from the juices of many kinds of learning and nothing in the present argument is intended to suggest any limit to the range of enquiry and speculation. Nor do scholars cease to be useful because their output is primarily aimed at other scholars. Much exploration of the seemingly irrelevant may be required in order to isolate what is actually relevant: a distinction on which scholars are no less entitled than practitioners to their own views. Altering the accepted bounds of relevance is an essential academic function.

The principle of utility is only repudiated when the theorist denies that his ideas will, even indirectly and through the mediation of others, help anybody to make a choice, to influence a choice or, no less important, to understand the choice made by somebody else. If he does so deny, he puts himself to the rather difficult proof that his ideas have any other value. Truth he can not claim, not in international relations. As Pascal long ago explained: '*vérité au deçà des Pyrénées, erreur au delà*'.[18] What is plausible for one country, one culture, one set of established interests and traditional preconceptions, can easily appear preposterous beneath an alien sky. Understanding and explanation can only be partial, in both senses of that adjective, and their extent is best demonstrated by their utility.

That theory should assist the understanding of choices is naturally a lesser objective than the one dismissed by Professor Reynolds – solving immediate policy problems – but it is both possible and desirable. It is possible, because some kind of theoretical concept, even if this is unconscious or disguised as 'experience', is present in every choice. It is desirable both for understanding the choices of others and for making one's own. In the first case, the assistance of theory is often indispehsable. No practitioner, for instance, can hope to understand Soviet policy choices without some acquaintance with the theoretical concepts of Marxist-Leninism. Nor is this an isolated example. All over the world are countries, under the most varied forms of government, in which the British diplomat must first penetrate the essentially theoretical concepts which form the background to policy-making, then, which is often more difficult, explain them to the Foreign Office. Both tasks are easier if the academic groundwork has been laid and both illustrate the principle that the utility of a theory does not depend on its abstract truth: if it influences choices, it is relevant.

The second case – assistance in making one's own choices – depends on a more controversial proposition: that a deliberately constructed and carefully argued theory stands a rather better chance than precedent, analogy, the memories of a vanished youth or instinctive prejudice, of escaping the common pitfalls of obsolescence, superficiality and conditioned response. It is only a rather better chance, because the nature of international relations dictates that there will always be conflicting theories; that none of these can be falsified otherwise than in implementation – seldom even then; and that theories are more often accepted or rejected because of their compatibility with prevailing political interests than because of the quality of the arguments advanced in their support.

This advocacy of the utility of theory is thus open to the objection, which will not be raised by practitioners alone, that it amounts to arguing that any theory is better than none. This is indeed the proposition here advanced. The multiplicity, actual and prospective, of theoretical concepts is no obstacle to their utility. On the contrary, it could well be argued that nothing has been more harmful to the practical conduct of international relations or, indeed, of any kind of politics, than the temporary tyranny of a single dogma. This has happened often enough during the twentieth century, in one country or another, to provide apparent justification for the pragmatic retort that it is better to have no theory at all. As this is impossible, in the sense in which theory is here understood, a conscious choice from different theories, even from various elements of each, may offer better prospects than unconscious reliance on a single prejudice.

But how is this selection to be made? The answer will not satisfy the theorists. The practitioner will be guided by his intelligence, his experience, his traditional preconceptions, his sense of political realities to choose those theoretical concepts which seem to him both to crystallise what he has vaguely thought and to offer him the words with which to convey his meaning to others. He will prefer the familiar and, if he is to be persuaded to consider the novel, he will demand both lucidity and relevance. Of course, it would greatly assist him in his choice if he shared a basic training with the theorists, if they shared his practical experience, if both had a common vocabulary. These are advantages enjoyed by doctors of medicine, but unfortunately denied to most practitioners of international relations.

They are, that is to say, in Britain. Other countries do favour a degree of professional training for their diplomats and in some of them there is a significant interchange of personnel between the official and the academic world. Not all these arrangements are ideal. The academics in the State Department are insufficiently numerous to compensate for the dilution of the American Foreign Service by political appointees whose inexperience is seldom matched by intellectual distinction. The integration of scholarship and bureaucracy in the Soviet Union might be considered excessive. But so, surely, is their divorce in Britain. If the 223 successful candidates for the administrative stream of the Diplomatic Service between 1964 and 1975 included only seven (none after 1975) who had graduated in international relations, something is wrong somewhere. The principle of utility is not finding its most obvious application.

Many explanations of this curious phenomenon – itself only one instance of a general British tendency to undervalue the practical utility of studying international relations – could be attempted. What is taught perplexes bureaucrats by differing from one university to another. More legitimately, they question the dearth of practical experience among the teachers – a professor of surgery who never performed an operation! Such arguments are naturally also excuses. The Foreign Office find a professionally unconditioned intelligence more plastic to the impression of their traditional preconceptions. To politicians their officials are sufficiently trying without the aggravation of academically certified theories.

The causes are not material to the present argument, but the fact remains. In Britain the study of international relations is not yet admitted as a useful, let alone an indispensable, preliminary to its conduct. It has been the purpose of this article to argue that it should be so accepted. This does not mean that those who teach international relations in the universities should regard as their primary task the preparation of candidates for the Diplomatic Service. Nor does it imply that the Foreign Office should cease recruiting graduates qualified in other subjects. Both scholars and practitioners have other tasks, and the understanding of policy choices – where their preoccupations coincide – is a relatively small area of intersection in two otherwise distinct spheres of interest. Nor are professional diplomats often the most important actors in a drama that tends to involve us all. Nevertheless, insofar as scholarship is concerned with the criteria of choosing, there is a case for ensuring that academic fruits are available to those involved in the act of choice.

It has always been a necessary condition for the emergence of a civilisation that some of its members should have time to think, to invent, to teach. For its survival it may be equally important that these lessons should be applied. This will not happen unless those who teach direct their efforts to the imparting of useful information. There are few subjects in which the connection between useful information and survival is more inescapable than in international relations. At present, in Britain, there is a gap between the academic study of international relations and its practical conduct.

The extent of this gap may be appreciated from a single example. Visitors to the British Ministry of Defence cannot help observing, in any office to which they are allowed access, the presence of publications from the International Institute for Strategic Studies. These are also to be found in other government departments, even the Foreign Office, where arguments deriving from these publications are bandied about. So they are in newspapers from Beirut to Helsinki. In the field of strategic studies, which ought to be a tributary of international relations, but which sometimes seems on the point of swallowing its suzerain, the utility of the academic contribution, however heretical, is fully recognised. Practitioners do not disdain the offerings of theory; relevance and utility are admitted principles; and scholars do not regard experience as an impediment to speculation.

When an equal understanding is achieved in the wider field of international relations, that subject will be generally accepted as what it actually is: one of the useful arts.

12 The Political Influence of the Thriller

> Come Miss Morland, let us praise Udolpho in whatever terms
> we like best. It is a most interesting work. You are fond of
> that kind of reading?
> To say the truth, I do not much like any other.
>
> Jane Austen[1]

Miss Morland's tastes are widely shared today, for Udolpho was an
early thriller, that is to say, a story of conflict or intrigue, nowadays
usually involving crime, espionage or violence, in which the reader's
attention is focused on the dangers run by the characters. There are
few forms of writing so clearly identifiable or which command a wider
public. In 1967, for instance, the world's 50 most frequently
translated authors included 11 writers of thrillers, of whom Simenon
surpassed Shakespeare and was beaten only by the heavily subsidised
Lenin, while Alistair Maclean did almost twice as well as George
Bernard Shaw.[2] In 1961, 25 per cent of all paperbacks published in the
United States were thrillers;[3] and in 1971 about a fifth of British
fiction in print as paperbacks fell under the heading of 'Murder and
Mystery'.[4]

These crude figures – there are no useful statistics of comparative
sales and readership – can be reinforced by ordinary observation.
Thrillers are more widely and easily available to the public than almost
any other category of book. Not only do most libraries and bookshops
reserve a special section of their shelves for thrillers, but these are
always prominent in the far more numerous bookstalls and miscel-
laneous shops that include among their other wares a small selection
of paperbacks. These distributors are responding to a special kind of
popular demand. The casual reader in search of distraction frequently
has no particular book in mind. He is likely to prefer fiction – a recent
survey suggests that this accounts for over half of all books borrowed
from public libraries[5] – but he does not ask for 'a novel', because

novels are too heterogeneous. He looks for an identifiable type of novel. If the reader is a man (women tend to prefer romances) his choice is most likely to be a thriller.

His tastes will be equally well served if he prefers watching to reading. In one week chosen at random nearly 50 per cent of all fictional entertainment programmes on British television were thrillers. As a means of communicating with a mass audience, the thriller probably offers greater opportunities than any of the conventional methods of disseminating political ideas. Party political broadcasts are often switched off before they begin, leading articles are skipped by most newspaper readers, political books and pamphlets seldom command a wide circulation. Indeed, overtly political ideas do not always attract much attention even among the minority actively interested in politics, many of whom are positively repelled by any expression of opinion which differs markedly from their own.

Exceptional talents or opportunities are needed if explicity political propaganda is to exercise much impact beyond the narrow circle of party workers and others already committed. Thrillers, on the other hand, have long been as popular among the politically influential as they are with the general public. Baldwin revelled in the works of Buchan;[6] two of his successors in the office of Prime Minister paid public tribute to Agatha Christie on her jubilee as a writer; President Kennedy was one of Ian Fleming's faithful readers; and many less illustrious politicians have been happy to confess to interviewers their addiction to so innocent and popular a form of relaxation.

Given the ease with which the thriller reaches both the masses and the ruling class, all that is odd about the idea of its political influence is that this should receive so little notice. In England, admittedly, writers of fiction are not taken very seriously. It is only, or so we believe, in the Soviet Union that the publication of *One Day in the Life of Ivan Denisovich* could constitute a major political event or the circulation of *Dr Zhivago* be treated as akin to treason. Yet English law recognises the ability of novels to influence those into whose hands they fall, by the occasional prosecution of authors for the explicit description of sexual behaviour, and English politicians have not always been indifferent to the impact of fiction. Gladstone, when Prime Minister, resorted to public denunciation of a short story: *The Battle of Dorking*. 'These things go abroad', he declared, and 'the result of these things is practically the spending of more and more of your money'.[7]

Political novels, even the most successful – *Animal Farm, On the*

Beach, *Fail Safe* – nevertheless arouse a certain consumer-resistance among that substantial section of the public (many of them not without political influence) who resent attempts at persuasion, shun anything 'serious' and demand 'a good read'. To them the thriller seems less suspect, a surer source of the pleasures of unadulterated escapism. This is precisely its attraction for the modern propagandist, who no longer alienates his audience by assertion and argument but, whether it is a cigarette or a politician he is selling, seeks to project an 'image' by appealing to emotions, prejudices and cravings as potent as they are often unconscious or unavowed.

For techniques of this kind the thriller is a natural medium. Unlike the old-fashioned detective story, which teased the reader's intelligence with a neatly packaged conundrum, the thriller is in the mainstream of imaginative literature: it seeks to arouse vicarious emotion. But excitement and suspense will only grip the reader who has first been induced to suspend his disbelief. The crude melodrama of the earlier writers no longer passes muster today, when readers and viewers expect a coherent plot and an authentic setting before they will surrender their critical faculties and identify their own emotions with those of the characters.

Ian Fleming, for instance, owed much of his success to the meticulous verisimilitude of his backgrounds. The precise detailing of Bond's breakfast helped us to swallow the octopus as well. Fleming's revelling in the minutiae of luxurious living was unjustly denounced as a superfluous snobbery. It was an essential element in his technique of suspending the reader's disbelief. Having introduced him to one unfamiliar, but interesting and easily comprehensible, aspect of a strange existence, Fleming leads him on, step by carefully detailed step, to the temporary acceptance of ever wilder fantasies, each anchored to seeming reality by an authentic address, a brand name, a specific price, a topical reference.

Even the cleverest handling of incidental detail is nevertheless insufficient to render plausible a story of crime, violence and suspense, unless these, and the sensational events they produce, are given a convincing social framework. In the earlier days of the thriller this framework had little political significance: the story was set in places or periods sufficiently unfamiliar for the strangest combinations of circumstances to be supposed probable by the unsophisticated. Such were the Gothic novels that so entranced Miss Morland, but her successors have long learned to heed Henry Tilney's exhortation to 'consult your own understanding, your own sense of the probable, your own observation of what is passing around you'.[8] There are still thrillers set on lonely islands or in isolated farm-houses, but they have to be very good – and the isolation has to be very plausibly explained – to exert the same impact today.

Besides, the more restricted the setting and the fewer the characters, the greater the ingenuity required from the writer in providing a sufficient variety of thrills to maintain suspense and excitement. Car-chases, the techniques of sabotage, frontier crossings, alien con-spiracies and the unforeseen interventions of passers-by: all these enrich the author's scope, but the more contact his characters have with the world around them, the more they commit him to a view of that world's political and social organisation. He must be prepared to answer – affirmatively and plausibly – Henry Tilney's key question: could such atrocities be perpetrated in a country like ours?

Raymond Chandler faced that question squarely, presenting a picture of a Californian society in which any degree of violence, cor-ruption and oppression seemed credible. Thrillers are read for enter-tainment, not for instruction, but we are nevertheless accustomed to accept much information on trust from their writers, because it is necessary for our enjoyment of the story. How many people not pro-fessionally interested in such subjects could honestly claim to know much more of legal and police procedures, toxicology or espionage than they have learned from thrillers? And learned, what is more, almost unconsciously, for the best thriller writers have a gift, which any instructor should envy, for conveying technical information both palatably and imperceptibly. But, if we believe Chandler when he tells us that paraffin wax will reveal traces on the hand that fired the fatal pistol, why should we not believe him on other subjects as well? Provided, of course, that his views appear (as they always do) to be no more than incidental to the main theme of the book.

For fantasy soon loses its grip on the educated reader. Once the book is finished, the spell is broken. He no longer accepts the super-human virtues, strength and acumen of the hero; the depravity of the villains or the plausibility of much of the intrigue. But he remembers the bit about paraffin wax and the return of his normal scepticism does not entirely obliterate the impression, conveyed with casual art, that Californian society is inimical to the more refined concepts of justice or civilisation.

Sophisticated Russians no longer admit to a belief in the contem-porary reality of Dickensian England, but one wonders how many British writers on the importance of violence in the American political scene have been influenced as much by Chandler and his imitators as by first-hand experience or more erudite reading. Historians, after all, have seldom scrupled to draw on the fiction of their period to supplement the aridities of their more respectable documentation. And the reader we are considering – the busy executive who relaxes over a thriller – may never in all his life open a book on the nature of Californian politics and society. On that, as on the climate and the characteristics of gunshot wounds, Chandler is his authority and the source, conscious or unconscious, of many of his reactions to the next headline or news flash from California.

Even so, Chandler does not take the thriller beyond the first stage of its political involvement: the creation of a setting appropriate to conflict and violence. Numerous writers have gone further and chosen a specifically political intrigue as the mainspring of their plot. Even when this is no more than international rivalry, its adoption entails a greater degree of political commitment. The readers of Ian Fleming and Alistair Maclean must identify themselves not only with the hero, but with his country, its allies and a particular conception of the world. Few Russians, Chinese or Communists could regard these works as novels of pure entertainment. Other writers prefer more complex forms of political conflict. Hurd and Osmond, in *Send Him Victorious* describe a *coup d'état* in Britain involving the kidnapping of the Monarch; Knebel and Bailey, in *Seven Days in May* expose an American President to similar plotting by the Joint Chiefs of Staff. Subversion of the established political order, whether the villains are domestic or foreign, has long been a traditional theme for the thriller.

Most writers handle it on the fairly simple assumption, which could be a reflection of the views of readers rather than an attempt to influence them, that the *status quo* is acceptable and its subversion a crime. Complications arise when the powers that be are infiltrated by the enemy or otherwise incapable of right action, so that the hero must actually struggle against authority to restore the just equilibrium. This often confronts him with the crucial questions: whom can he trust, who is the ultimate custodian and interpreter of the national interest? It is striking how often, nowadays, this father-figure turns out to be some kind of secret policeman. This was less true of an earlier generation, when the heroes of Buchan, Sapper and Leslie Charteris made up their own minds and allowed established authority only a secondary and often derisory role.

Curiously enough, the change seems to have come from the Left. The early novels of Graham Greene – *A Gun for Sale, It's a Battle-*

field, *Confidential Agent* – depict a social order as fundamentally and generally corrupt as Chandler's, but still discern a residual virtue in the British police. In Nicholas Blake's *The Smiler with the Knife*, the heroine finds the Head of the Special Branch her only ally in foiling a Fascist *coup d'état*. Eric Ambler's British heroes relied on an illegal resident of the KGB to assist their struggle against appeasement and the sinister machinations of international capitalism. The trend has since spread across the political spectrum – John le Carré's ambivalence is now exceptional – and reaches its height in the sophisticated and idiosyncratic works of William Haggard, who takes a differently jaundiced view of British society. The Foreign Office, diplomats and civil servants are regularly flayed in his pages; those British politicians whom he likes or, more often detests are – very recognisably – allotted supporting roles or sticky ends; the *Daily Express*, the Americans and the KGB are invariably treated with respect. But the nation's only saviour – the arch father-figure of them all – is Colonel Russell of the Security Executive.

The final stage of political involvement is attained when the thriller becomes the vehicle of a specific message on a political issue of topical importance. It is always dangerous to speculate about the motives of imaginative writers and, the higher the quality of their work, the harder it is to guess whether a particular subject was chosen for its literary or its propagandist attractions. But the political impact of *The Riddle of the Sands* is as well established as that of *The Quiet American*, Constantine Fitzgibbon's *When the Kissing Had to stop* was a powerful argument against the Campaign for Nuclear Disarmament, then at the height of its influence, while John le Carré's *A Small Town in Germany* was equally topical in its warning against the dangers of Neo-Nazism. Only Graham Greene's masterpiece, admittedly, was far enough ahead of existing currents of opinion to be regarded as a major source of new ideas. Other writers, however, have enlisted the thriller in support of even more unorthodox views. That remarkable novel, *The Douglas Affair*, by Alistair Mair, is a saga of insurgent Scottish Nationalism in which the villains are English politicians and the Special Branch.

Overt commitment, particularly to minority causes, nevertheless remains a rarity in the thriller. It is not necessary to its political influence. Indeed, as earlier argued, it may even constitute an impediment. That influence is most reliably based on one of the fundamental postulates of the thriller: the menace that can only be met by force, the wrong for which society provides no legal remedy. Even that embodiment of the enlightened social conscience, the schoolmaster hero of Michael Gilbert's enthralling *Fear to Tread*, has to resort to blackmail to defeat a highly placed villain whom the police are powerless to prosecute. Most writers are less scrupulous: to them power grows out of the barrel of a gun.

Even when the ultimate success of violence is reassuringly diverted to the safe hands of heroes and of authority, this is a doctrine of great political potency. Obviously it coincides with the moral climate of our times, but no amount of research is ever likely to determine how far thrillers merely reflect that climate or to what extent they help to create it. Thrillers have been shown to command a wide audience and to be suitable vehicles for the unobtrusive dissemination of the political concepts that are at least implicit in most of them. The intriguing question is whether or not this potential is, or might be, deliberately exploited. The artist – and many writers of thrillers are of outstanding talent – is admittedly an uncertain instrument in the hands of the propagandist. However discreetly tempting the inducements – and the author of thrillers has a special need for the authenticity which official information can give – the result may only be a masterpiece as remote from the intentions of the client as a portrait by Graham Sutherland. Even the bestseller has his own integrity and a considerable independence. Some scope there must be for suggestion and persuasion: the political spectrum of the thriller is wide enough for most propagandists to pick a writer who need only vary and enrich his accustomed themes. But authors able and willing to diffuse a message that was not of their own devising might best be sought among those of lesser talent, many of whom already earn their living by embroidering the ideas of others: the script-writers for films and television, the ghosts of stock serials, the already compliant servants of editors and producers and publishers. Someone, after all, skilfully reversed in the film of *The Quiet American* the political message of the book. Do the carefully authentic *romans policiers* of television owe only their factual knowledge, or also their ethos to official assistance? Had those who tunnelled into that bank so suggestively close to Baker Street actually read *The Mystery of the Red-Headed League*? Which subversive group is now studying, as diligently as the Abwehr in 1940, the works of our leading authors?

To the student of politics these are questions not altogether devoid of interest. To the sociologist they offer opportunities for research. To authors, one suspects, they may at most suggest a plot and to addicts they will surely seem irrelevant. The art of the thriller will outlive its political implications and adrenalin will be demanded even when it is adulterated.

Notes and References

Chapter 1   Coercion, Compromise and Compliance

1. Keijo Korhonen (ed.), *Urho Kekkonen: A Statesman for Peace* (Otava Publishing Co., 1975) p. 30.
2. Lord Home, *The Way the Wind Blows* (Collins, 1976) p. 161.
3. Sir Anthony Eden, *Full Circle* (Cassell, 1960) pp. 136–8.
4. Home, op. cit., p. 293.
5. See Grant Hugo, *Appearance and Reality in International Relations* (Chatto and Windus, 1970) for a fuller exposition of this concept.
6. Edward Gibbon, *History of the Decline and Fall of the Roman Empire* (Chatto and Windus, 1875) p. 31.
7. Hannes Jonsson, *Friends in Conflict: The Anglo-Icelandic Cod Wars and the Law of the Sea* (C. Hurst, 1982).
8. Quoted in George Hills, *Rock of Contention* (Robert Hale, 1974) p. 226.
9. Marshal Mannerheim, *Memoirs*, trans. Lewenhaupt (Cassell, 1953) p. 375. Even this admirable statesman was not entirely immune to the mildew of cant, as witness his comment on the British declaration of war: 'a sign that morality no longer had any meaning in high politics' (p. 438).
10. See James Cable, *Gunboat Diplomacy 1919–79*, 2nd edn (Macmillan, 1981) pp. 36–9.
11. Ibid., Ch. 2, for further elucidation of this concept.
12. *Hansard*, vol. 529, cols 428–550, and Victor Bator, *Vietnam: A Diplomatic Tragedy: Origins of US Involvement* (Faber and Faber, 1967) p. 113.
13. See Cable, op. cit., passim.
14. Henry Kissinger, *Years of Upheaval* (Weidenfeld and Nicolson, and Michael Joseph, 1982) p. 148.
15. Evelyn Waugh, *Scott-King's Modern Europe* (Chapman and Hall, 1947) p. 88.
16. Vladimir Dedijer, *The Road to Sarajevo* (MacGibbon and Kee, 1967) p. 327.
17. Frederick Forsyth, *The Devil's Alternative* (Hutchinson, 1979).

Chapter 2   The Diffusion of Maritime Power

1. Admiral Stansfield Turner USN, quoted in James A. Nathan and James K. Oliver, *The Future of United States Naval Power* (Indiana University Press, 1979) p. 48.
2. International Institute for Strategic Studies (IISS), *The Military Balance 1981–1982*.

3. Quoted in James Cable, *Gunboat Diplomacy 1919-1979*, 2nd edn (Macmillan, 1981) p. 145.
4. Cable, ibid., p. 248.
5. Robert L. Scheina, 'The Argentine Navy Today', *Naval Forces*, vol. II, no. 1 (1981) pp. 34-5.
6. Cable, op. cit., p. 246.
7. Bradford Dismukes and James McConnell, *Soviet Naval Diplomacy* (Pergamon Press, 1979) pp. 130-3.
8. Arthur J. Marder, 'The Royal Navy and the Ethiopian Crisis of 1935-36', *American Historical Review*, vol. LXXV, no. 5 (June 1970).
9. Captain A. T. Mahan, *The Influence of Sea Power upon the French Revolution and Empire 1793-1812* (Sampson, Low, Marston, Searle and Rivington, 1892) p. 118.
10. IISS, op. cit.
11. Lord Strang, 'Essay on the Formation and Control of Foreign Policy' in *The Diplomatic Career* (André Deutsch, 1962).

Chapter 3   Interdependence: a Drug of Addiction?

1. As such it can be employed by both parties to a dependent relationship

> for those who wish the United States to retain world leadership, interdependence has become part of the new rhetoric, to be used against economic nationalism at home and assertive challenges abroad (Robert O. Keohane and Joseph S. Nye, *Power and Interdependence* (Little Brown, Boston, 1977) p. 7)

2. Thomas Babington Macaulay, *Frederic the Great* (Longman, Brown, Green and Longmans, 1855) pp. 30-1.
3. Lyon Playfair, *Subjects of Social Welfare* (Cassell, 1889) p. 307. Lyon Playfair, a Scot, was Edinburgh Professor of Chemistry, a protégé of the Prince Consort, a constant gadfly, a MP, a Minister and ultimately a Peer (1818-98).
4. Sir Robert Ensor, *England 1870-1914* (Oxford University Press, 1936) p. 106.
5. Ibid., p. 227, and Andrew Shonfield, *British Economic Policy Since the War* (Penguin, 1958) p. 255.
6. Playfair, op. cit., p. 234.
7. Ibid., pp. 335-6.
8. See, for instance, that brilliant if profoundly depressing book *The Collapse of British Power* (Methuen, 1972) by Correlli Barnett.
9. Playfair, op. cit., p. 141.
10. Ibid., p. 283.
11. R. F. Harrod, *The Life of John Maynard Keynes* (Macmillan, 1951) pp. 426-30.
12. John Maynard Keynes, *The Economic Consequences of the Peace* (Macmillan, 1919) p. 238.
13. Ian H. Nish, *The Anglo-Japanese Alliance* (Athlone Press, 1966) p. 221.

14. A. J. P. Taylor, *English History 1914–1945* (Pelican, 1970) p. 221.
15. Harold Nicolson, *King George V* (Constable, 1952) p. 463.
16. Radio broadcast of 9 February 1941.
17. Margaret Gowing, *Independence and Deterrence: Britain and Atomic Energy 1945–1952*, vol. I: *Policy Making* (Macmillan, 1974) p. 185.
18. These undertakings, as described to Parliament by Mr Heseltine on 1 February 1983, are not, in any case, of a particularly impressive character. President Truman reaffirmed in 1952 'the understanding that the use of these bases in an emergency would be a matter for joint decision of Her Majesty's Government and the United States Government in the light of circumstances at the time' (*The Times*, 2 February 1983).
19. Michael M. Harrison, *The Reluctant Ally: France and Atlantic Security* (Johns Hopkins University Press, 1981) p. 179.
20. *Defence in the 1980s: Statement on the Defence Estimates 1980*, vol. I (HMSO) Cmnd 7826-I, p. 9.
21. Ibid., p. 32.
22. Captain John O. Coote RN, 'Send Her Victorious', *United States Naval Institute Proceedings*, January 1983.
23. James Cable, *The Royal Navy and the Siege of Bilbao* (Cambridge University Press, 1979) p. 180.
24. M. W. Kirby, *The Decline of British Economic Power Since 1870* (George Allen and Unwin, 1981) p. 136.
25. Magnus Clarke, *The Nuclear Destruction of Britain* (Croom Helm, 1982) passim.
26. Bernard Ledwidge, *De Gaulle* (Weidenfeld and Nicolson, 1982) p. 227.
27. Ibid., p. 383.
28. *The United Kingdom and the European Communities* (HMSO, July 1971) Cmnd 4715, para. 56.
29. Compiled from the relevant tables in *Economic Trends – Annual Supplement 1982* (Central Statistical Office, HSMO, 1982).
30. Richard E. Caves and Lawrence B. Krause, *Britain's Economic Performance* (The Brookings Institution, Washington, 1980) p. 11.
31. Field Marshal the Viscount Montgomery of Alamein, *Memoirs* (Collins, 1958) p. 505.
32. The addiction, perhaps this is not too strong a word, of this article to the outcome of predictions as the test of argument should not be construed as unreserved endorsement of the scientific approach to political problems. This has pitfalls which even Lyon Playfair did not escape, as in his comment on the great Irish Famine of 1847–8:

> As the population lessened, the production of potatoes per acre decreased.... The reason for the decline is curious...the best manure for any crop is the refuse of the animal which lives upon it...when the people emigrated they took their manurial value with them, and the diminished population did not supply sufficient manure for the crops. (Thomas Wemyss Reid (ed.), *Memoirs and Correspondence of Lyon Playfair* (P. M. Pollak Science Reprints, Jemimaville, Scotland, 1976) p. 100)

Chapter 4   Will Gibraltar be Next?

1. *Guardian*, 14 August 1982.
2. George Hills, *Rock of Contention* (Robert Hale) p. 382.
3. Argentine delegate to the UN in 1965; Spanish statement of 1966.
4. House of Commons, 'Seventh Report from the Foreign Affairs Committee Session 1980–81' (HMSO), 22 July 1981, para. 149.
5. *Keesing's Contemporary Archives*.
6. Barry Wynne, *The Day Gibraltar Fell* (Macdonald, 1969).

Chapter 5   Diplomacy: a Case for Resuscitation

1. 'Diplomacy is the management of international relations by negotiation; the method by which these relations are adjusted and managed by ambassadors and envoys; the business or art of the diplomatist' (Harold Nicolson, *Diplomacy*, 3rd edn (Oxford University Press, 1963) p. 15).
2. T. S. Eliot 'The Hollow Men', *Poems 1909–1925* (Faber and Faber, 1925) p. 127.
3. Grant Hugo, *Britain in Tomorrow's World* (Chatto and Windus, 1969) p. 27.
4. Christopher J. Makins, quoted in William Wallace and W. E. Paterson, *Foreign Policy Making in Western Europe* (Saxon House, 1978) p. 51.
5. Central Policy Review Staff (CPRS), *Review of Overseas Representation* (HMSO, 1977) p. 2.
6. Ibid., p. 48.
7. Expenditure Committee of House of Commons, *Fourth Report* (HMSO, 7 March 1978) vol. II, p. 303.
8. Geoffrey Moorhouse, *The Diplomats* (Jonathan Cape, 1977) p. 151.
9. *Webster's New International Dictionary*, 3rd edn.
10. William Wallace, *The Foreign Policy Process in Britain* (Royal Institute for International Affairs, 1975) pp. 270–1.
11. CPRS, op. cit., passim.
12. Wallace, *The Foreign Policy Process*. p. 1.
13. William Wallace, 'After Berrill: Whitehall and the Management of British Diplomacy', *International Affairs*, vol. 54, no. 2 (April 1978).
14. See note 5.
15. 'I got the impression that here was a man who could be relied upon when he had given his word' (Chamberlain after his first meeting with Hitler: Telford Taylor, *Munich: The Price of Peace* (Hodder and Stoughton, 1979) p. 743). Roosevelt, who believed that some of his career diplomats were 'working for Winston', concluded from his first meeting with Stalin: 'That's our big job now, and it'll be our big job tomorrow, too: making sure that we continue to act as referee, as intermediary between Russia and England.'
    The mirror-image of this notion, cherished by successive British leaders, only adds to the ironies inherent in the diplomacy of the brief encounter (see Elliott Roosevelt and James Brough, *A Rendezvous with Destiny* (W. H. Allen, 1977) pp. 362–3).

16. Thirty years ago the accepted treatment for general paralysis of the insane was to infect the patient with malaria, the resulting rise in temperature being the curative agent. In that case, however, the induced malaria, once its work was done, could itself be cured by quinine. In international relations this is the kind of therapy that doctors describe as 'heroic'. See James Harpole, *A Surgeon's Heritage* (Pan, 1953) p. 170.
17. Speech in the House of Commons, 11 November 1947.

Chapter 6   The Falklands Conflict

1. 'Four Principles of 11 February 1918', in Harold Nicolson, *Peacemaking 1919* (Constable, 1944 edn) pp. 40–3.
2. Secretary of State for Defence, *Statement on the Defence Estimates 1966* (HMSO) Cmnd 2907, p. 10.

Chapter 7   Surprise in the Falklands

1. *Daily Telegraph*, 26 June 1982.
2. In 1971 the Iranian Navy seized the strategically important islands of Greater and Lesser Tumb at the mouth of the Persian Gulf. In 1974 China seized the Paracel Islands in the South China Seas; South Vietnam in the same year took the Spratley Islands, which were retaken in 1976 by the Vietnamese Liberation Navy; and Turkey invaded and occupied Eastern Cyprus. In 1975 Indonesia invaded and occupied East Timor.

Chapter 8   Surprise and the Single Scenario

1. There were also 50 British sailors landed from the small sloop HMS FAVOURITE. See V. F. Boyson, *The Falkland Islands* (Oxford University Press, 1924) pp. 61–3.
2. Interview with Miss Oriana Fallaci, *The Times*, 12 June 1982.
3. Boyson, op. cit., pp. 66–7.
4. General Robert Close, *Europe without Defence* (Pergamon, 1979) pp. 153–98.
5. *Statement on the Defence Estimates 1982* (HMSO) Cmnd 8212-I, p. 29.
6. Ibid., p. 25.
7. *Hansard*, House of Lords, Monday, 20 July 1981, vol. 423, col. 121.
8. *Statement on the Defence Estimates 1980* (HMSO) Cmnd 7826-I, p. 32.
9. *The Way Forward* (HMSO, June 1981) Cmnd 8288, p. 11.
10. See Chapter 7.
11. See Chapter 4.
12. John Terraine, *To Win A War* (Sidgwick and Jackson, 1978) p. 14.
13. Ibid.

Chapter 9 Cant in Foreign Policy

1. Boswell, *Life of Johnson*.
2. Marshal Bulganin to Sir A. Eden, 5 November 1956, quoted in Anthony Eden, *Full Circle* (Cassell, 1960) p. 554.
3. *Documents relating to British Involvement in the Indo-China Conflict* (HMSO, 1965) Cmnd 2834, doc. 45.
4. Thomas Babington Macaulay, *Historical Essays*.
5. Cmnd 2834, op. cit., doc. 84.
6. Sir E. Goschen to Sir E. Grey, quoted in Guy Chapman, *Vain Glory* (Cassell, 1937) pp. 5–6.
7. Harold Nicolson, *Lord Carnock* (Constable, 1930) p. 334.
8. G. P. Gooch and H. Temperley, *British Documents on the Origins of the War*, vol. VIII (HMSO, 1926–38). Mr Eyre Crowe of the Foreign Office had written a memorandum on 15 November 1908 concerning British obligations towards Belgium, which concluded:

   > Great Britain is liable for the maintenance of Belgian neutrality whenever either Belgium or any of the guaranteeing Powers are in need of, and demand, assistance in opposing its violation.

   On which Sir Charles Hardinge, then Permanent Under-Secretary, minuted:

   > The liability undoubtedly exists as stated above, but whether we could be called upon to carry out our obligation and to vindicate the neutrality of Belgium in opposing its violation must necessarily depend on our policy at the time and the circumstances of the moment. Supposing that France violated the neutrality of Belgium in a war against Germany, it is, under present circumstances, doubtful whether England or Russia would move a finger to maintain Belgian neutrality, which [*sic*] if the neutrality of Belgium were violated by Germany it is probable that the converse would be the case.'

   This observation the 'morally unassailable' Sir Edward Grey found 'to the point'.
9. Nicolson, op. cit., p. 420.
10. Ibid., p. 419.
11. Ibid., p. 416.
12. A. J. P. Taylor has explained that 'by suffering he meant only the interruption of British trade with the continent of Europe'. See A. J. P. Taylor, *The Struggle for Mastery in Europe* (Oxford University Press, 1954) p. 530.
13. Statement to Congress as reproduced in Robert S. McNamara, *The Essence of Security* (Hodder and Stoughton, 1968) p. 76.
14. Speech by President Johnson on 7 April 1965 as reproduced in Cmnd 2756 (HMSO, 1965) doc. 21.
15. Winston Churchill, *Their Finest Hour* (Cassell, 1944) p. 107.

16. McNamara, op. cit., p. 4.
17. Carte, *History of England*, quoted in the *Oxford English Dictionary* as an early example.
18. It is curious how similar phrases recur on the lips of belligerence – compare the earlier quotation from President Johnson: 'the surest road to peace'.
19. *The Penguin Hansard* (Penguin Books, 1940) p. 11.
20. *Hansard*, 14 December 1932, vol. 273, col. 354.
21. McNamara, op. cit., p. xii.
22. For a fuller exposition of this thesis see Grant Hugo, *Britain in Tomorrow's World* (Chatto and Windus, 1969).

Chapter 10   Hong Kong: a Base Without a Fleet

1. Harold Nicolson, *Curzon: The Last Phase* (Constable, 1939) p. 13.
2. Admiral of the Fleet Sir Edward H. Seymour, *My Naval Career* (Smith Elder, 1911) p. 326.
3. Palmerston's verdict quoted in Nigel Cameron, *The Cultured Pearl* (Oxford University Press, Hong Kong, 1978) pp. 18–19.
4. Captain Charles Elliott RN quoted in G. B. Endacott, *A History of Hong Kong* (Oxford University Press, Hong Kong, 1973) p. 14.
5. Seymour, op. cit., p. 326.
6. For relations with Japan generally see Ian H. Nish, *The Anglo-Japanese Alliance* (Athlone Press, 1966) and *Alliance in Decline* (Athlone Press, 1972).
7. Grace Fox, *British Admirals and Chinese Pirates* (Kegan Paul, Trench, Trubner, 1940) p. 46.
8. *The Times*, 1 October 1982.
9. Ibid., 23 September 1982.
10. Not that Britain is idle in this respect. *The Times* reported on 18 January 1982 that new premises were being constructed in Hong Kong for the GCHQ station presumably dedicated to monitoring China.
11. *The Times*, 7 October 1982.

Chapter 11   The Useful Art of International Relations

1. J. N. Rosenau, *The Scientific Study of Foreign Policy* (Free Press, 1971) p. 21.
2. John Ziman, *Reliable Knowledge* (Cambridge University Press, 1978) p. 42.
3. Quoted in Robert L. Pfaltgraff, Jr, 'International Studies in the 1970s', *International Studies Quarterly*, March 1971.
4. 'Kaiser Wilhelm's great ambition, fired by his reading of Mahan... was to create as large a navy as possible' (Paul M. Kennedy, *The Rise and Fall of British Naval Mastery* (Allen Lane, 1976) p. 214).
5. William L. Shirer, *The Rise and Fall of the Third Reich* (Fawcett Crest, 1966) pp. 152–9.

6. In the Cuban missile crisis of 1962 (see Robert F. Kennedy, *13 Days* (Macmillan, 1968) p. 65).
7. J. M. Keynes, *The General Theory of Employment Interest and Money* (Macmillan, 1936) Ch. 24 v.
8. Ibid.
9. *Theory and Policy in International Politics* (Open University Press, 1975) pp. 72, 59.
10. Karl W. Deutsch, 'On Political Theory and Political Action', *American Political Science Review*, March 1971, p. 22.
11. Richard Nixon, *US Foreign Policy for the 1970's: A Report to the Congress, Feb. 9, 1972* (Washington: US Government Printing Office) p. 2.
12. H. J. Mackinder, 'The Geographical Pivot of History', record of a paper read at the Royal Geographical Society on 25 January 1904, *The Geographical Journal*, vol. XXIII, no. 4 (April 1904).
13. Lord Strang, 'Essay on the Formation and Control of Foreign Policy' in *The Diplomatic Career* (André Deutsch, 1962) pp. 115–16.
14. Ibid., pp. 119–20.
15. 'Traditionalism Versus Science in International Relations', in Morton A. Kaplan (ed.), *New Approaches to International Relations* (St Martin's Press, 1968).
16. G. L. Goodwin, 'Theories of International Relations', in Trevor Taylor (ed.), *Approaches and Theory in International Relations* (Longman, 1978) p. 302.
17. Vladimir Dedijer, *The Road to Sarajevo* (Simon and Schuster; MacGibbon and Kee, 1966) p. 327.
18. Blaise Pascal, *Pensées et Opuscules* (Hachette, 1909) Section V, no. 294, p. 465.

Chapter 12 The Political Influence of the Thriller

1. Jane Austen, *Northanger Abbey* (J. M. Dent) p. 87.
2. UNESCO, *Statistics of Authors Most Frequently Translated* (1! 7).
3. Robert Escarpit, *The Book Revolution* (Harrap, 1966).
4. Whitaker, *Paperbacks in Print* (1970–1).
5. Peter H. Mann, *Books, Buyers and Borrowers* (André Deutsch, 1971) *passim*.
6. Colin Watson, *Snobbery with Violence* (Eyre and Spottiswoode, 1971) p. 210.
7. I. F. Clarke, *Voices Prophesying War, 1763–1983* (Oxford University Press, 1966).
8. Austen, *Northanger Abbey*, p. 163.

Index

Index